Lake District

William Forrester

photography by

Barry Stacey

HarperCollins*Publishers*

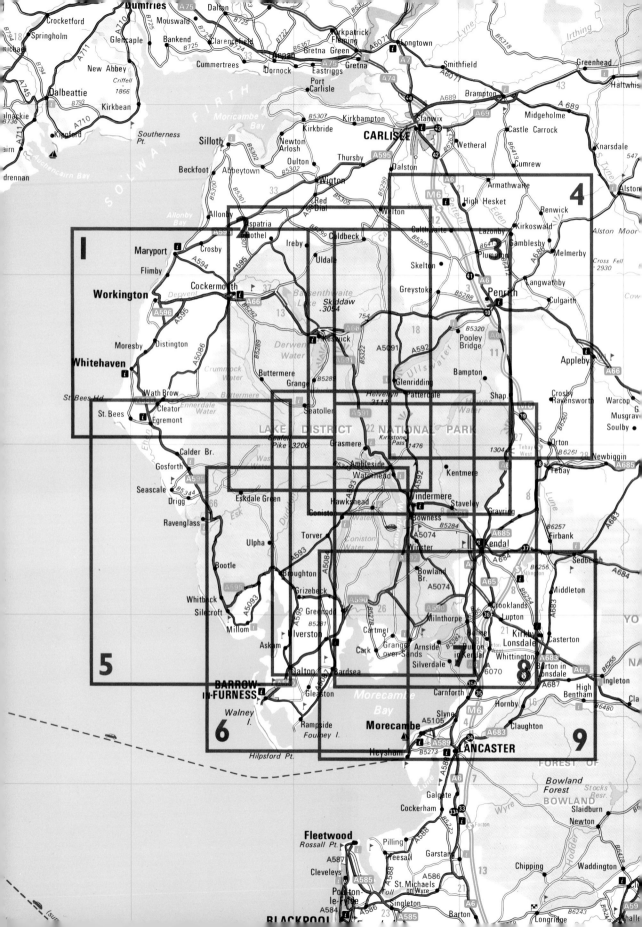

CONTENTS

Carling Knott, Loweswater

St Begas's church, Bassenthwaite

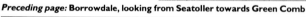
Preceding page: **Borrowdale, looking from Seatoller towards Green Comb**

There is a lot of variety in this small area – to the east are craggy mountains and well-loved lakes, and to the west a gently undulating plain stretching to a coastline teeming with docks and industry. And yet even amid this comparative ugliness, you'll find plenty of charming surprises, such as the isolated and ancient town of St Bees.

You can't really understand the north-west or the district as a whole unless you look at its geology. The oldest rocks, at 500 million years, are found around Bassenthwaite. Called Skiddaw slates, they are not the type to roof your house with, because they break too easily. This slate wears away quickly too, so the mountains here have fine, smooth profiles. The mountains south of Buttermere are altogether different and made of harder, craggier volcanic rock laid down about 450 million years ago. To the west and under Workington, Maryport and Whitehaven are 300 million-year-old coal measures. St Bees is different again, with great red sandstone cliffs formed some 230 million years ago.

Industry isn't something one usually associates with the Lakes and yet this region used to be a major industrial area. Whitehaven, for example, was once the second largest port in the country after London. The town owes much of its rich

Maryport

Winter storm, Bassenthwaite Lake

St John's church, Buttermere

history to its industrial past and has much to offer the visitor. By the mid 19th century, 200,000 tons of coal were being produced here annually and the pits eventually extended for 3 miles (5 km) under the sea. Other industries gradually sprang up, using both local and imported materials to produce detergent, sulphuric acid, cement and, of course, iron. The iron went to make cannons and ships. The wealth generated by all this trade and industry led to the importation of luxury items such as tobacco, spices, rum and sugar from the West Indies. It is hardly surprising that many of the local recipes seem very rich. A classic example is Cumberland Butter. This used to be a traditional

gift for a newborn baby: the Demerara sugar represented sweetness, the nutmeg and cinnamon zest, the butter a smooth path through life and the rum, of course, spirit!

Naturally, such prosperity was acquired at a cost to both people and the natural landscape. Coal-mining has always been a disfiguring and potentially dangerous business – Whitehaven, for example, lost 136 men and boys in a pit explosion in 1910 and a further 104 in 1947. Still, anyone with a feel for history will find plenty hereabouts to interest them.

Other signs of old industry can be found inland. The disused workings of the Buttermere and

Workington Castle

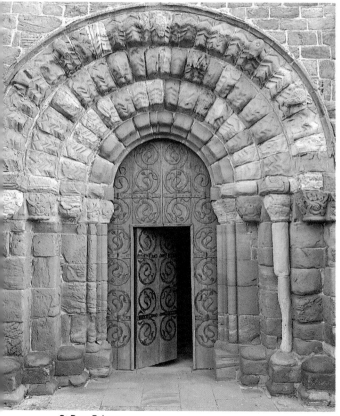

St Bees Priory

Buttermere

Westmorland Green Slate Company can still be seen at Honister Pass. The road from the west winds up beside the old tramway which moved slate mined from underground quarries called 'close heads'. Black powder was used to blast down to a depth of some 700 feet (225 m); gelignite would have shattered the slate totally. Large blocks of the green slate were brought up to be cut by diamond-tipped saws and then split and shaped in time-honoured fashion by hand. Only 10 per cent of the mined rock could be used. The rest was abandoned on 'spoil heaps', making a mess of the countryside.

Forestry is another controversial industry that has had an impact on the area. After World War I the new Forestry Commission decided that the bare hillsides in the Lake District could be made

St Bees Head

productive. The result was heavy-handed planting of conifers around Ennerdale Water and instant outrage among those who value Lakeland for its open views. The Commission has changed its views over the years and in the last decade the 13 miles (20 km) of Sitka spruce planted at Ennerdale have been mellowed by the addition of larch and broad-leaved trees.

This area of Lakeland is teeming with wildlife. At Bassenthwaite, a wildlife site of special scientific interest, you'll see rare plants and birdlife, and a fish (the vendace) so rare in England that the only other place you'll find it is in Derwentwater next door. A little farther on, at St Bees, is the only place in England where the black guillemot breeds.

The scenery is superb too. Buttermere wowed many early visitors to the Lakes and remains a

9

Whitehaven harbour

Honister Pass, looking towards High Stile

firm favourite. Fortunately, vehicles these days aren't defeated by the steepness of Honister Pass and you won't, as they used to, have to get out of your vehicle at this point and walk. The Lakes were toured for their views and yet most of these early visitors didn't want to see them as they really were. They'd turn their backs and gaze at the scenery through their hand-held Claude glasses, which tinted and framed every scene. Natural beauty was not appreciated for its own sake in those days but had to be brought up to certain aesthetic standards and 'improved upon'. Looking

at the views is still the most common visitor activity in the Lakes, but nowadays without the Claude glasses.

The Lake District has such a sorry reputation weather-wise that you've probably been wondering whether you'll see the scenery at all. Seathwaite has the dubious distinction of being this country's wettest inhabited spot, with an annual rainfall of 130 inches (325 cm). This doesn't mean that it is always raining here, just that you get a lot of rain at one go; 6 inches (15 cm) a day is not uncommon. The rainfall is exceptional because of

Wordsworth memorial, Cockermouth

Cockermouth

Above Crummock Water

Footpath, Crummock Water

Seathwaite's situation. The rainclouds are forced to rise by the mountains and, as a result, deposit their contents on the village below. The mountain tops excepted, which have a very harsh climate for most of the year, the rainfall in other parts of the region is about average for the country as a whole. The weather really does vary a great deal within a short distance. Grange, for example, is just a few miles from Seathwaite and has a dry, mild climate similar to Torquay's. If it's raining in your valley or dale, take the advice of the locals and try another one! 11

❶ BUTTERMERE

The walk around the lake gives superb views. One of the great scandals of the 19th century involved Mary Robinson, the Beauty of Buttermere. She thought she'd married the Earl of Hopetoun's brother only to discover that her husband was a bankrupt imposter. He was hanged and she later married a local farmer.

❷ COCKERMOUTH

This small, ancient market town is Wordsworth's birthplace. Wordsworth House (Main Street), the Georgian mansion where the poet spent his childhood, has been faithfully restored by the National Trust. The garden is especially lovely. (Open Apr–4 Nov daily; Sun afternoons only) The Castlegate House Gallery (Castlegate Drive), built in 1739, contains Georgian sculpture, paintings and glass. (Open Mar–Dec, Mon–Wed and Fri–Sat) Those who like a bit more action will find it at the Cumberland Toy and Model Museum (Market Place), a fine collection of mainly British toys of the last 100 years. Among the many working toys is a large, vintage Hornby layout. Special exhibitions are held each year. (Open Feb–Nov daily ☺) ☎ Phone 0900 822634

For something completely different, go to Wythop Mill, Embleton (just 4 miles/7 km along the Bassenthwaite road). Here you'll see the old sawmill's overshot wheel and an exhibition of old woodworking machines. Coffee shop. (Open Easter–Oct, Sun–Thurs. Phone 07687 76394)

❸ CRUMMOCK WATER

This lake is fed by two of the local sights: Scale Force and Loweswater. Scale Force is just to the west of the lake; at 172 feet (52 m) it is the highest waterfall in a district famous for them. To reach it, take the rough footpath from Buttermere. Far less strenuous are the walks at Holme Wood, on the west side of Loweswater.

❹ DALEHEAD BASE

Displays, craft days and guided walks are run here by the National Park. Refreshments available. (Open Apr–Sept daily. Phone 07687 77294) You can reach Honister Pass (1176 ft/359 m) from the base and nearby there is a side road which branches off to the tiny hamlet of Seathwaite. From here you can walk to Stockley Bridge and the 140-foot (43 m) cascade of Taylor Gill Force.

❺ ENNERDALE WATER

A wild, remote and peaceful spot. Take the forest trail from the car park and viewpoint at Bowness Knott (north side of the lake).

❻ MARYPORT

The docks which once played a major role in this town's prosperity are now being restored as a boat haven. One of the attractions is the *Flying Buzzard*, a 1951 Clyde tugboat. (Open Easter–Oct, Thurs–Tues ☺ ☺) The Maritime Museum (Senhouse Street) tells the story of local boatbuilding and of two local lads: Fletcher Christian (of *Mutiny on the Bounty* fame) and Thomas Ismay (founder of the White Star shipping line). (Open Easter–Oct, Mon–Fri, Sat morning and Sun afternoon. Nov–Apr, Mon–Tues and Thurs–Sat) ☎ 0900 813738

❼ MIREHOUSE

This 17th-century house east of Bassenthwaite Lake has a fine collection of furniture, paintings and literary items. In the grounds you'll find the Norman church of St Bega, the Old Sawmill Tearoom and four adventure playgrounds! The grounds lead down to Bassenthwaite Lake, according to Tennyson the final resting place of King Arthur's sword, Excalibur. (Open Apr–Oct: grounds daily, house afternoons only ☺. Phone 07687 72287)

❽ ST BEES

This town manages to combine scenic beauty and history. The church here used to be part of an ancient priory (founded c 650 AD). Don't miss the superb Norman door (1160) at the west end. The public school nearby dates back to 1583. You can reach the lighthouse by walking north of the car park in the town and up the sandstone cliffs of St Bees Head (462 ft/90 m).

❾ THORNTHWAITE GALLERY

A 300-year-old building displaying works for sale by local artists. In summer there are demonstrations of individual crafts. Tea room. (Open mid Mar–Nov, Wed–Mon ☺ �&. Phone 059682 248) North-west of the Swan Hotel is the Bishop of Barf, a 7-foot (2 m) high whitewashed rock.

❿ WHINLATTER VISITOR CENTRE

The main feature of the Centre is an exhibition which tells the story of the forest. There are also displays, picnic facilities, refreshments and a forest trail. The top of Whinlatter Pass offers superb views. (Open Feb–Dec daily &. Phone 059682 469)

⓫ WHITEHAVEN

Whitehaven was one of England's busiest ports in the 18th century and a target of pirates. Whitehaven has some superb Georgian buildings; look at the houses at the point where Roper Street meets Scotch Street, or at the church. The Museum and Art Gallery (Market Place, in the Civic Hall) has model ships, mining displays and lots of gruesome detail about a very well preserved 14th-century battle casualty who was dug up recently at St Bees. (Open Mon–Sat) Michael Moon's bookshop (Roper Street) is a mecca for many and has its own mini museum/gallery at the rear, room for 100 browsers and one mile of shelving. (Open Mon–Sat; closed Bank Hols &) ☎ 0946 695678

⓬ WORKINGTON

This maritime and coal town's most famous visitor was Mary Queen of Scots, who stopped over at Workington Hall after fleeing Scotland in 1568. A series of storyboards helps you explore what remains of this once great country house. (Open Easter–Oct, Mon–Fri; Sat–Sun, afternoons only) For local history, go to the small Helena Thompson Museum, in Park End Road. (Open Mon–Sat. Phone 0900 62598)

The Northern Lakes

Preceding page: **Early morning, Derwentwater**

Moot Hall, Keswick

Watendlath

St John's Vale, Keswick

Thirlmere

Judith Parr's House, Watendlath

Many visitors choose to use this area as their base for exploring the whole of the Lake District. Quite simply, for most Lakeland enthusiasts Derwentwater is *the* lake, Langdale *the* valley and Watendlath *the* hamlet. The scenery is classic too – the north dominated by the rounded slopes of the Skiddaw range, and the south by the craggy, wild central Lakeland mountains.

The town of Keswick separates the two distinctive areas of Skiddaw and Borrowdale. Skiddaw, the region's third highest peak (3053 ft/931 m) lies just a few miles north of Keswick. The 'grandpa' mountain of the Skiddaw slate group, it is composed of softer, crumblier rock than that found to the south at Borrowdale, where the brasher, newer, tougher volcanic rocks dominate the heart of Lakeland.

These newer rocks, forced up by heat, are rich in minerals. The discovery of one of the strangest of them, graphite, led to the development of the pencil industry in the area. The graphite was made by a process involving trees being caught in lava and then crushed for many millions of years. Some people say it's a pity the process didn't continue a bit longer and produce diamonds instead! All the same, graphite has turned out to be of tremendous importance to the area. At first no one could work out how it might be used. The locals tried burning it, with little success, then they marked sheep with it instead. Later it was found to be just the thing for dusting your cannonball moulds if you wanted the casting to come out perfectly. Others swore by it as a sure cure for all sorts of digestive problems. The demand for graphite eventually became so great that, by 1788, it was fetching over £3,300 a ton. It was said that a mouthful of 'wad' (the local name for the mineral) smuggled out of the mine would buy you drinks for a week at the Queen's Hotel in Keswick. When graphite was sent to London, it was by armed stagecoach. Someone eventually discovered that graphite is ideal as a writing and drawing material and, as a result, a thriving cottage industry in artists' pencils sprang up in Keswick. The pencil industry still goes on in the town. The mining of graphite, though, sharply declined after 1795 when a way was found of manufacturing the mineral artificially.

Ironically, Keswick also has a close association with an organization that's about as far removed from mining as you can get – the National Trust. Canon Rawnsley, the local vicar, was one of the

Castlerigg Stone Circle, Keswick

Crossthwaite church, Keswick

founder-members of the Trust, which he helped to set up in 1895. He was the Trust's honorary secretary until his death in 1920. Rawnsley fought tirelessly to get the 195 acres of Brandelhow Woods and Fell for the Trust in 1901, raising £7,000 in five months. This was the first National Trust property in the Lakes. In 1922 Friar's Crag and the surrounding area were bought as a memorial to the canon. Since this time the Trust's landholdings in the area have grown to include most of the central fell area, almost all the major valley heads, six of the main lakes, 86 farms, several campsites, numerous car parks and, last

Barrow Bay, Derwentwater

Nichol End, Derwentwater

Jaws of Borrowdale, Derwentwater

but by no means least, a cottage with an earth privy. (The cottage is being preserved and is let to visiting tourists.)

Unfortunately, Canon Rawnsley didn't win all his battles. Despite the help of such heavyweight contemporaries as William Morris, John Ruskin and Thomas Carlyle, Rawnsley couldn't prevent Manchester Corporation passing a law (1879) which allowed the water level of the two natural lakes of Thirlmere to be raised by 54 feet (16 m) and turned the area into one vast reservoir. The project flooded the old road and the hamlets of Armboth and Wythburn. Also lost was the bridge which joined the two lakes and which the poets Coleridge and Wordsworth had often used as a meeting point. Wythburn church – a favourite spot from which to start the climb up Helvellyn – survives. You can see pictures of the area as it looked before the flooding at the King's Arms pub at Thirlspot.

The locals were even less happy in 1908 when the hillsides were densely planted with conifers to control soil erosion and the speed that rainfall ran off into the lake. More recently the North-West Water Authority (the new owners) have been planting native trees again and allowing people

19

John Peel's grave, Caldbeck

Snow-capped Skiddaw

Little Langdale Tarn

Ashness Bridge

both around and on the reservoir, so Thirlmere is coming to life again.

Hunting is a favourite pastime in the region. Britain's most famous huntsman, John Peel, lived and died in Caldbeck, a village the other side of the Skiddaw range from Keswick. He's best remembered as the hero of the song, 'D'ye Ken John Peel' (1828/9), which was written one snowy afternoon by Peel's friend John Graves, whose daughter wanted to know the words to a song her grandmother was singing. Graves did no more than pen a new set of words in honour of his friend, who was with him at the time. Graves's old house is marked with a plaque to commemorate the event. The song was given its first public airing in the Rising Sun Inn, Caldbeck, now called the Oddfellows Arms.

Caldbeck

Whatever your views on foxhunting, Peel was a bit of a character. A big man (over 6 feet tall and weighing about 13 stones), he had a large nose, tremendously long legs and very sharp grey eyes. 'His coat so grey' was, of course, made of local undyed Herdwick wool. After eloping to Gretna Green, he spent the rest of his life neglecting his family and farm for the greater pleasures of the hunt and hostelry. One less than complimentary local described him as, 'Nobbut a drunken old tagglet'. Maybe he had some excuse, though. After all, Caldbeck did have 13 pubs in those days.

Peel hunted foxes obsessively. On one occasion, he's reputed to have gone on for 10 hours 40 minutes without a break – all in vain, though, because his quarry escaped. Peel died as he had lived – hunting.

21

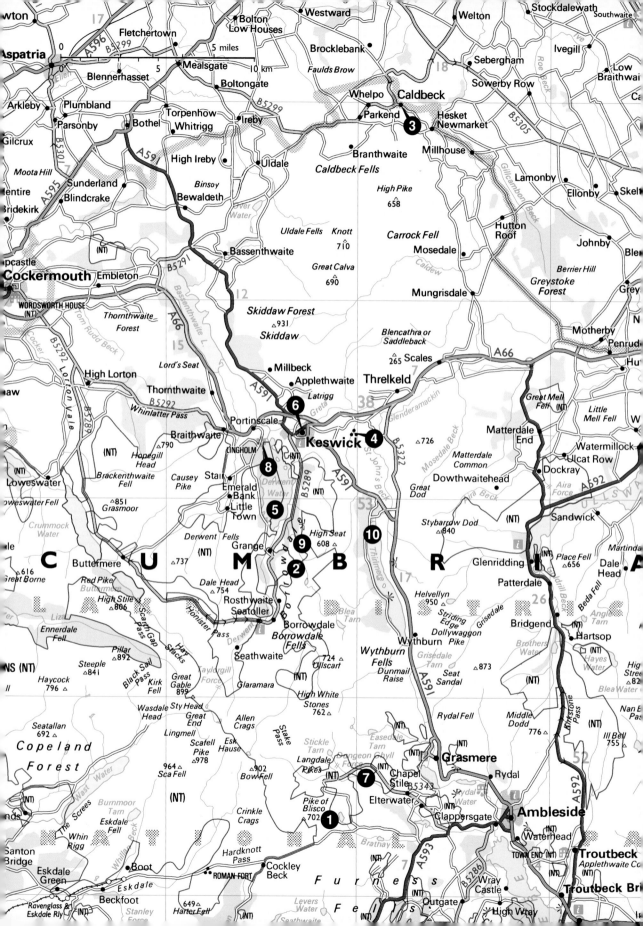

❶ BLEA TARN

There are several small, picturesque lakes called Blea Tarn in the Lake District. Wordsworth loved this particular Blea Tarn, and I'm sure you will too; you can walk right round the lake. In *The Excursion* he wrote:

'Full many a spot
Of hidden beauty have I chanced to espy
Among the mountains; never one like this;
So lonesome, and so perfectly secure'.

❷ BORROWDALE

This valley lies just to the south of Derwentwater. Don't miss the exceptionally pretty village of Grange. Near here the valley narrows into the 'Jaws of Borrowdale' and to the west is the easily accessible Castle Crag viewpoint. To the east you'll find the massive Bowder Stone. It looks as though it's about to topple over any minute, but don't worry – it's been keeping its balance since the Ice Age! The Stone is 36 feet (11 m) high, 62 feet (19 m) long, weighs about 2000 tons, and you can climb to the top of it.

❸ CALDBECK

This was the stamping ground of the huntsman John Peel. Born at Park End, Caldbeck, in 1776, he was finally laid to rest in Caldbeck churchyard in 1854. His gravestone, decorated with hunting motifs, is still there. Also in Caldbeck you'll find Priest's Mill, an 18th-century watermill with its machinery fully restored and in working order. There's a small mining museum and a coffee shop here too. (Open mid Mar–Sept, Tues–Sun; Oct, Thurs–Sun; Nov–Dec, Sat and Sun only ♿. Phone 06998 369)

❹ CASTLERIGG STONE CIRCLE

It is not known why the present 38 boulders were erected some 3500 years ago in this superb setting. The 'circle' is actually an oval, 107 feet (33 m) across at its broadest point. ♿

❺ DERWENTWATER

A favourite with many people, this lake can be explored by launch from Lakeside. Alternatively, you can walk on just a bit farther south to Friar's Crag, where you'll find what John Ruskin considered to be one of the finest views in Europe. Castle Head, just north-east of here (across the B5289), also offers a rewarding view.

❻ KESWICK

The town's four museums provide plenty of variety. Cars for the Stars features the motors of Del Boy, Bergerac, James Bond and the Saint. (Open Mar–Dec daily ♿ ☕) The Railway Museum (Main Street) gives the history of the Cumbrian railway. (Open Easter–Oct daily, afternoons only) The Cumberland Pencil Museum (Greta Bridge) tells the story of pencils through the ages. Exhibits include the world's longest pencil, at 7 feet (2 m). (Open Mar–Oct, Mon–Fri; Sat–Sun afternoons only ♿ ☕) The Keswick Museum and Art Gallery (Fitz Park) houses the original manuscript of *Goldilocks and the Three Bears* as well as weird curiosities such as a 500-year-old mummified cat or the so-called musical stones, a 12-foot (3.5 m) long musical instrument you can have a bash at playing. (Open Apr–Oct, Mon–Sat ♿) ☎ 07687 72645

❼ LANGDALE

This popular area has lovely scenery and many enjoyable walks. Most visitors head west from Great Langdale and stop at either the National Trust car park for Stickle Ghyll or the car park by the New Dungeon Ghyll Hotel to explore both waterfalls. Stickle Ghyll Force drops 128 feet (38 m) onto boulders. Dungeon Ghyll Force is named after the black chasm that the waterfall (52 ft/16 m) plunges into. Farther up the valley is Old Dungeon Ghyll Hotel, which was given to the National Trust by the famous historian G. M. Trevelyan. If you're not feeling very energetic but want a bit of peace and quiet, try walking up the valleys of Mickleden Beck or Oxendale Beck. Behind Fell Foot Farm, in Little Langdale (on the way to Wrynose Pass), there's a flat-topped mound with steps leading up to it. This is thought to be a Thing Mount or Assembly Mound for the Vikings who once ruled this area.

❽ LINGHOLM

Lingholm has impressive formal gardens, woodland and great views. Beatrix Potter's family used the house as a holiday home for a few years and Lingholm itself crops up in many of the writer's tales. Tea rooms and plant centre. (Open Apr–Oct daily ♿. Phone 07687 72003) Lingholm woods were Squirrel Nutkin's home. Just north, at Fawe Park is Benjamin Bunny country. To the south is Newlands Valley and the setting for Mrs Tiggy-Winkle. She lived up the side of Cat Bells, a popular fell walk. This is best reached from Gutherscale car park (just north-east of Skelgill), or from Hawse End pier which connects with the Derwentwater launch.

❾ LODORE FALLS

You'll find these next to the Swiss Lodore Hotel. Small cascades splash through rocks in the woods and then drop 40 feet (12 m). If you want to see the Falls 'smiting and fighting', in Robert Southey's memorable words, make sure you visit them after heavy rainfall. Barely a mile north of here is a side road leading to Ashness Bridge, Surprise View and Watendlath (the tiny, isolated village that was the home of Hugh Walpole's Judith Paris). All three are beauty spots and consequently are crowded in summer. Leave your car behind and use the Derwentwater launch instead; this will set you down at Ashness bridge pier.

❿ THIRLMERE

This reservoir serves Manchester, some 96 miles (150 km) away, and stretches along by the side of the main Keswick to Grasmere road. The road along the west side is the more peaceful route. There are good viewpoints at Raven Crag (north-west end of lake) and Hause Point (a promontory two-thirds of the way along the lake). Between them lies Launchy Ghyll Forest Trail and its 100-foot (30 m) high waterfall.

Wordsworth Country

Stone bear, Dacre churchyard

Preceding page: Gowbarrow Bay, Ullswater   Dacre Castle

The name of the poet William Wordsworth is inextricably linked to the heart of Lakeland. He spent his whole life here and drew inspiration for his greatest works from it. The Lakes have a literary tradition that begins with Wordsworth and continues to this day.

The classic portrait of Wordsworth has him walking for miles through the Lakeland countryside – with his favourite mountain, Helvellyn, in the background – composing at the top of his voice. One of the poet's friends, the writer Thomas de Quincey, reckoned that Wordsworth had walked some 180,000 miles (288,000 km) during his lifetime.

Wordsworth was born at Cockermouth in 1770 (see page 13) and brought up, much to his disgust, in Penrith. He went to grammar school at Hawkshead (see page 77) and then on to be a lazy undergraduate at St John's College, Cambridge. By 1791 he'd become a radical as a result of his visits to revolutionary France.

Wordsworth and his sister Dorothy went to live

Rydal Water

Brotherswater Inn

Loughrigg Tarn, near Ambleside

at Dove Cottage, Grasmere, in 1799. Life was quite hard at this time – porridge was often on the menu and newspaper served as wallpaper. When their financial situation eventually eased, William married his sweetheart, Mary (1802). The wedding left his sister in a state of collapse. 'Poor Miss Wordsworth', as she was called locally, later went mad. William, in contrast, faired considerably better. It was at this time that he started producing some of his best work, including *Daffodils*; in fact, for this poem William drew on raw material

supplied by Dorothy, who had kept detailed descriptions of the flowers they had seen during a walk two years earlier.

The Dove Cottage era ended in 1808 when William and his growing family moved to Allan Bank, also in Grasmere. They all hated it. The house was cold and the chimneys smoked; William called it 'a temple of abomination'. (Allan Bank was given to the National Trust by Canon Rawnsley but is not open to the public.) Understandably, the family soon moved again, in 1811, 27

View across Ullswater to Gowbarrow Fell

Ullswater

Grasmere

Outward Bound School sailing boat, Ullswater

Clappersgate Bridge, near Ambleside

Dove Cottage

but their choice was not a fortunate one. The damp Grasmere parsonage was the scene of the deaths of Catherine and Thomas, two of the Wordsworths'- five children. Two years later, in 1813, the family settled in Rydal Mount, a short distance from the parsonage. William, now financially secure in a government job as distributor of stamps, parted company with his radical past. He returned to the fold of the Anglican church and the establishment, becoming a Tory, opposing the 1832 Reform Bill and eventually, in 1843, becoming Poet Laureate. He died on 23 April 1850.

The tradition of rushbearing dates back to the days when churches had earth floors covered with rushes. Once a year the rushes were changed – no doubt greatly improving the odour of sanctity. The churches in the area now have tiled or flagged floors, but several communities continue to mark the occasion. The modern version of this ancient

Ullswater from near Howtown

ceremony is a much grander affair than the original. In Grasmere and Ambleside, for example, it's a great family occasion complete with processions and bands.

Dates: Grasmere Rushbearing is on the Saturday nearest 5 August (St Oswald's Day). Ambleside Rushbearing is a movable feast but is usually held on the first or second Saturday in July. Warcop, Musgrave and Urswick also hold rushbearings. If you can't arrange to see one, have a look at the mural in Ambleside Church for a glimpse of the proceedings.

Children who attend Rushbearing at Grasmere and Ambleside are given pieces of the region's 29

Martindale

Ambleside by Stock Ghyll

Aira Force, Ullswater   **Water wheel at Stock Ghyll**

Glenridding Pier, Ullswater

Pooley Bridge, Ullswater

spicy gingerbread, which is a bread- or cake-like sweet rather than a biscuit.

Such a diet would undoubtedly help you to become as large as a certain George Steadman, though whether you would be as fit is another matter. Steadman was fourteen times heavyweight champion in Cumberland and Westmorland wrestling at the Grasmere Games in the 19th century. His chest measured 51 inches (128 cm) across and his calves were almost 18 inches (47 cm) round. This type of wrestling is similar to sumo. The two opponents clasp hands behind each other's back and necks and try to force each other to touch the ground or release the hand-hold. Bouts are generally won with a crafty flick, so agility and intelligence are needed more than brute force and weight. The various flicks have wonderful names such as the hank, the swing hype or the cross-buttock. The last of these terms was invented by the rector of Egremont! To add to the spectacle the wrestlers wear what looks like thermal underwear topped with velvet knickers. Hot stuff on a summer's day.

An equally strenuous Lakeland summer sport is fell running, which involves running up and down a mini mountain. The fell-running competition held at Grasmere is called the 'guides race'. Contestants have to leap down scree, scramble over walls and scratch themselves skinless on the heather. Great fun!

If that doesn't appeal, why not try hound trailing instead? This is designed to let man's best friend do the hard part and leave you to pick up the prize and the praise at the end. The hounds are specially bred and fed for the event; the diet being a closely guarded secret. To make them eager, they are starved for the 24 hours immediately prior to the race. The race begins when the hounds are let loose (or given 'the slip') to follow a specially laid paraffin and aniseed trail. This may wend and wind for up to 8 miles (12 km) before leading them back to the start. The owners are in a frenzy of excitement during the closing stages of the race, their enthusiasm no doubt fuelled by the bets that hang on the result.

This and similar traditional sports are held at Ambleside on the Thursday before the first Monday in August. At Grasmere on the third Thursday after the first Monday in August, you can enjoy high leaping, long leaping and flat racing. If you find it too complicated working out the date, phone the Tourist Information Centre!

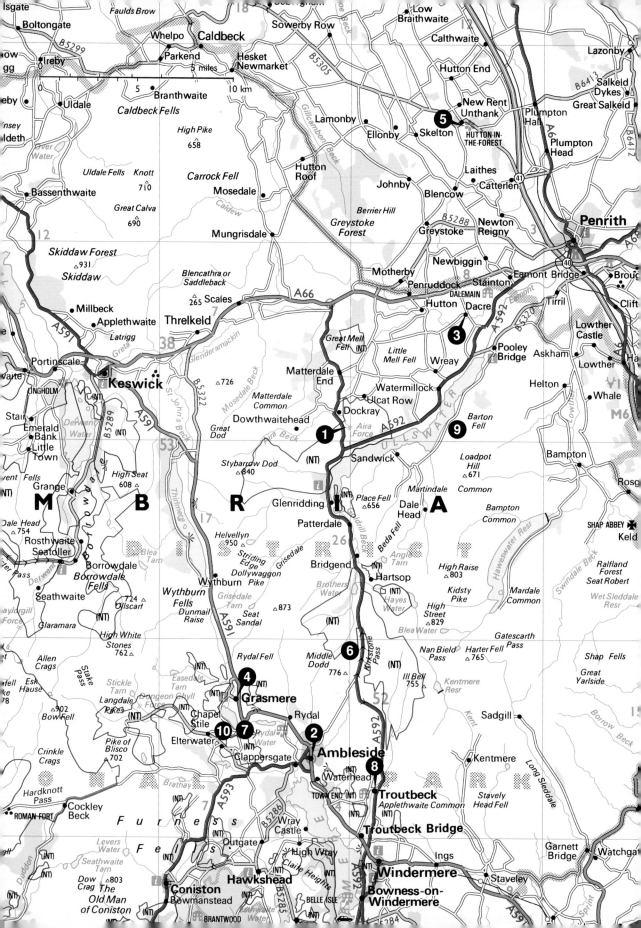

❶ AIRA FORCE

This famous 70-foot (21 m) high waterfall belonging to the National Trust stands in the grounds of the Victorian-landscaped Gowbarrow Park.

❷ AMBLESIDE

The heavy traffic and narrow pavements here are not conducive to a peaceful wander. However, Ambleside does have some delights. A unique and valuable collection of literature, the Armitt Collection, can be seen in a special section of the public library. (Open Mon–Wed and Fri) The art of glass-blowing is demonstrated at Adrian Sankey's Glass. (Open daily &) Nearby and perched precariously over the rushing waters of Stock Ghyll is Bridge House (c 1650). In the 1850s Mr and Mrs Rigg and their six children lived here – some feat considering that the main room of the tiny one-up, one-down summerhouse measures only 13 ft × 6 ft (4 m × 1.9 m)! Now the building is home to a National Trust shop and information centre. A walk to north-east Ambleside will take you to the 90-foot (27 m) Stock Ghyll Force waterfall. South-west of Ambleside are the foundations of a Roman fort, Galava. South-east of the town is Stagshaw Gardens, a National Trust property overlooking Windermere. (Open Apr–Jun daily; Jul–end Oct by appointment only. Phone 05394 32109) Behind the gardens stands the Jenkin Crag viewpoint (750 ft/230 m), which can be reached from Ambleside. ☎ 05394 32582

❸ DACRE

This village is steeped in church history; in 731 AD Bede wrote of a monastery in the village. The present church is Norman. In the churchyard are four weird carvings of bears. From the churchyard you can also see the 14th-century Dacre castle, which is said to be haunted but, unfortunately, is not open to the public.

❹ GRASMERE

You'll find plenty to do here. To the south-east of the village you'll find Dove Cottage and the Grasmere and Wordsworth Museum. William's years spent here (1799–1808) were the happiest and most productive of his life. Manuscripts, paintings, displays on local life and a mock-up of an old farmhouse interior are just some of the features. (Open Apr–Mar daily; closed Nov and Grasmere Sports Day &) In the village centre is St Oswald's Church, which has the graves of William, his wife Mary and his sister Dorothy. Nearby is Sarah Nelson's gingerbread shop – sweet-toothed visitors won't be able to pass by without sampling Sarah's famous recipe. There's a perfumery in the village and the Heaton Cooper Studio with its exhibition of paintings, including many watercolours of the lakes and mountains. (Open daily; closed Sun in winter &) Demonstrations of handloom weaving can be seen at Reekie's Limited. (Open daily &) If you want a breath of fresh air, head north-west out of the town and towards Easedale. This will bring you up past the waterfall of Sour Milk Ghyll to Easedale Tarn. From here you can walk up Helm Crag (1299 ft/396 m). ☎ 09665 245

❺ HUTTON-IN-THE-FOREST

This was reputedly the home of Sir Gawain's Green Knight, one of the characters in the tales of King Arthur and the Knights of the Round Table. More recently, since 1600, it has been the home of the Inglewood family. Although part of the house dates from the 1300s, the interior is Victorian. Outside there is a terrace of topiary, a walled garden, 'a forest walk and landscaped parkland. (House and tearoom open Jun–Sept, Thurs, Fri, Sun and Bank Hols. Grounds open all year, Sun–Fri. Phone 08534 449)

❻ KIRKSTONE PASS

There are two routes leading up to the Pass (1489 ft/454 m): one via an A road from Troutbeck and one via a steeper, unclassified road (called the Struggle) from Ambleside. Both routes provide good views. Just before you reach the top of the Pass, you'll come to the Kirkstone Pass Inn, which has the distinction of holding third place in the altitude ratings for English pubs. The Pass owes its name to a rock at the top which looks like a church steeple. The road to Ullswater takes you passed the lake of Brotherswater, allegedly named after two brothers who drowned here in a skating accident. Patterdale, a village famous for its late-summer sheepdog trials, stands almost at the edge of the lake.

❼ RYDAL WATER

This small lake has a Wordsworth haven to the north-east of it, Rydal Mount. The only colour portrait of the poet's sister, Dorothy, hangs in the house. The garden was planned by Wordsworth himself. (Open daily; closed Tues in winter. Phone 05394 33002)

❽ TROUTBECK

The main attraction of this village, apart from its setting, is Town End. Built about 1626 by a yeoman farmer called George Browne, this house was lived in by successive generations of the Browne family until 1944. It is full of the family's furniture, tools and artefacts. (Open Apr–Nov, Tues–Fri, Sun and Bank Hols. Phone 05394 32628) If you head south along the main valley road you'll come to Holehird Gardens, which has fine displays of azaleas, rhododendrons, alpine plants and heathers. (Open daily &. Phone 09662 4743)

❾ ULLSWATER

You can take a cruise on the second largest lake (7 miles/11 km long) in the area aboard either *The Lady of the Lake* (1877) or *The Raven* (1889), both operated by the Ullswater Navigation and Transit Company Ltd (of Kendal). Services run daily (early Apr–Oct &) from Glenridding to Howton and then on to Pooley Bridge. ☎ 07684 82414

❿ WHITE MOSS COMMON

This area lies between Grasmere and Rydal. A path leads from the car park to the River Rothay. Across the river you'll find a nature trail and paths leading to Loughrigg Terrace viewpoint and, for the energetic, on to Loughrigg Fell (1101 ft/336 m).

The North-East Lakes

Bridge at Lazonby

Pele church tower, Great Salkeld

Preceding page: **Haweswater from Mardale Common**

The old red sandstone town of Penrith is a wonderful centre for the visitor to this part of Lakeland. To the east and north there's the lush Eden valley; to the south there are many pretty limestone villages which gradually give way before the wilds near the summit of Shap's granite; and to the west scenery dominated by craggy volcanic rock.

Peace and quiet are, of course, just the thing for wildlife and especially birdlife. In the woods around Haweswater you'll find woodpeckers, pied flycatchers, redstarts, tree pipits and wood warblers, while by the lakeside itself there are dippers, grey wagtails and common sandpipers.

Up on the fells, wheatears and ring ouzels nest. Of the predators, there are sparrowhawks, buzzards, peregrine falcons and ravens, and the occasional golden eagle. In Haweswater itself there is an unusual silver fish called the schelly which grows to about 12 inches (31 cm) and is sometimes called the freshwater herring; other than here the schelly is only found in Ullswater and Red Tarn on Helvellyn. The char, a relation of the trout, is another regional rarity. On land, keep your eyes open for red squirrels, the shy roe deer, red deer and otters, which are making a comeback after a prolonged period of low numbers.

The region has a wide variety of plantlife.

Blacksmith's forge, Penrith Steam Museum

Long Meg and Her Daughters, Little Salkeld

Dalemain House

Alpines can be found high up on the mountains. It may seem curious that flowers are more scarce on the milder lower fells, but the competition from sheep and bracken can be too much, especially as the soil is often poor. In damp spots you may find plants that overcome this problem, such as the white sundew or the violet butterwort; both feed by trapping insects. Lower down the hillsides is juniper and bilberry country.

Yellow was appropriately the favourite colour of one of the district's most flamboyant characters – 'Hughie', fifth Earl of Lonsdale between 1880 and 1944, and a member of the Lowther Clan. The Lowthers were granted lands in Lakeland by

Edward I, in 1283, and went on to become tremendously wealthy; the development of White-haven was mainly due to their efforts. In the 1780s the family asked the Adam brothers to design Lowther village, intended to house their estate workers, but the project was only partially com-pleted. Lowther Castle, near Penrith, was another matter. This enterprise cost £60,000 and the remains of Shap Abbey, which was plundered for building stone. The house had an imposing 420-foot (128 m) frontage and was in the Gothic style. Such a grand setting called for grand entertaining and grand spending. Hughie was certainly equal to the task. His guest list included Edward VII and

37

Askham church

Howtown

Lowther Park

Wet Sleddale Reservoir, Shap

the Kaiser. Sixty servants would be on hand to wait on these and other illustrious visitors. It's hardly surprising that Hughie's annual expenditure in 1910 was £180,000.

The sport-mad Hughie became internationally famous when he challenged and subsequently beat the then world heavyweight boxing champion, John L. Sullivan. He was famous at home, too – for instituting the yellow Lonsdale Belt awarded in boxing, and for travelling in style in a yellow

Shap Abbey

Rolls-Royce and attended by yellow-liveried servants. Hughie was the Automobile Association's first president, hence the yellow uniform which was chosen in deference to him.

The 1930s saw a dramatic slump in the family's traditional source of income, coal mining, but no corresponding decrease in Hughie's spending. By the time of his death, in 1944, the Lowthers' financial affairs were in a parlous state and it was not until James, the seventh Earl, succeeded to the title in 1953 that the family's fortunes began to pick up again. Indeed, James ended up one of the country's richest men.

Lowther Castle was damaged by fire in the 1950s and later demolished to leave what remains today, an empty shell. The present Lord Lonsdale lives down the road from the old house, in the Elizabethan Askham Hall.

Lady Anne Clifford is a similarly remarkable

Maulds Meaburn

Near St Andrew's churchyard, Penrith

Shop sign, Penrith

character who has left her mark on the region. Her one misfortune was in being born a woman in 17th-century England. Marriage to the spendthrift and philanderer Richard Sackville, Earl of Dorset, became one long battle of wits for what she regarded as her inheritance – large tracts of land in the region. Sackville was quite as eager as Anne's male relatives that she should renounce her claim, because he would then receive a much-needed injection of cash in compensation for the loss of the lands; in those days what was hers was, in fact, his! But Anne gamely stuck to her guns, despite emotional pressure by her husband, who denied her access to her only child, and hectoring by the Archbishop of Canterbury and King James I. Eventually, her claim was rejected and that seemed to be that. The unhappy Anne buried Richard and then married Philip Herbert (later Earl of Pembroke), who wasn't much of an improvement on her first husband. But, by 1650, Philip too was

Crosby Ravensworth

Lowther Castle

Brougham Castle

Countess's Pillar, near Brougham

dead and Anne's male relatives had died, leaving her free to head north and take possession of what she'd fought for in vain all those years ago. Her life from this point on was like that of a medieval prince and was spent rebuilding the Clifford castles. She did this with great style, travelling from castle to castle with a retinue of about 300 servants. Her great courage did not lessen with age either. She remained openly and defiantly Royalist when most people daren't even whisper criticism of the Roundheads. As you'd expect, her sense of honour was no less robust. It's said that a fellow called Murgatroyd once refused to hand over a hen in payment of rent that he owed to the Clifford estate. Anne spent £200 pursuing the stubborn Murgatroyd through the law courts. After winning the case, she promptly sweetened the pill for Murgatroyd by cooking the pricey hen and asking him to eat it with her. Anne Clifford died in Brougham Castle, near Penrith, in 1676, aged 86.

❶ ACORN BANK GARDEN

This two and a half acre National Trust property lies about 6 miles (10 km) east of Penrith, at Temple Sowerby. Acorn Bank is noted for its herb garden; over 250 different varieties are grown here. (Open Apr–early Nov daily. ♿ to herb garden only. Phone 07683 61893)

❷ BROUGHAM CASTLE

The castle stands 1½ miles outside Penrith. Built in the early 1200s, it was one of the many castles restored in the 1600s by Lady Anne Clifford. It's in a super setting, on the River Eamont. You can climb the keep. There used to be a Roman fort nearby, hence the display of Roman tombstones. (Open Apr–Sept daily; Oct–Mar closed Mon. Part ♿ ⛴. Phone 0768 62488) Close to the castle is the ruined Brougham Hall. All that remains is St Wilfred's chapel. One mile east of the castle, on the A66, is the Countess's Pillar, which is decorated with brass sundials and commemorates the spot where Lady Anne Clifford last saw her mother alive.

❸ DALEMAIN

There's something for all the family at Dalemain House, which is part medieval, part Tudor and part Georgian. Inside the house you'll find fine paintings, furniture and an exotic Chinese room as well as displays on the local cavalry regiment, countryside and the local fell ponies. Outside there's a garden and adventure playground. (Open Easter–early Oct, Sun–Thurs ♿ ⛴. Phone 07684 86450)

❹ HAWESWATER

Another of the Lakeland reservoirs that supplies Manchester, this reservoir was begun in 1929 with the building of a 94-foot (29 m) high dam and the flooding of the village of Mardale; the latter makes the occasional unscheduled re-appearance in very dry summers. This isolated part of Lakeland is ideal for wildlife. An observation post is open in summer, when golden eagles nest here. (Phone 09313 337 or 376)

❺ HOWTOWN

Howtown is fabulous for walks.

For an easy one-hour meander, take the footpath round Hallin Fell. If you don't mind a short sharp climb (about half an hour's worth) to a viewpoint, climb the 1271-foot (391 m) fell itself. This is reached from the south side via a footpath which starts near the car parks by Martindale new church (between Howtown and Martindale). For a more energetic walk taking about four hours, leave your car at Glenridding, cross to Howtown by steamer and then return via the footpath that skirts the shores of Ullswater. An alternative circular walk involves parking the car at Martindale, walking up Boardale and over the pass at the top. You return north-west along the Ullswater shore path.

❻ LONG MEG AND HER DAUGHTERS

These form a massive (c 300 ft/92 m) stone circle. Long Meg is a 9-foot (2.75 m) tall standing stone. Twenty-seven of her original 59 'daughters' surround her. Legend has it that they were all turned to stone for dancing on Sundays!

❼ LOWTHER LEISURE PARK

All the fun of the fair in a 150-acre parkland setting. The many attractions include a circus, a BMX bike track, a deer park, an assault course, a boating lake, a miniature railway and an archery area. Many of the sights are under cover. This is also the venue for the Lowther Horse Driving Trials and Country Fair in early August. (Open Easter hols daily; mid Apr–Spring Bank Hol, weekends only; Spring Bank Hol–early Sept daily ♿ ⛴. Phone 093 12523)

❽ MAULDS MEABURN

This is a particularly beautiful village about 4 miles (6 km) east of Shap and well worth a visit.

❾ NUNNERY WALKS

The Walks are delightful if you are in the mood for a peaceful amble. They consist of 2 miles (3 km) of paths which take you through unspoiled woodland by the River Eden and then on to the waterfalls at the sandstone gorge of the River Croglin. Tearoom. (Open daily

♿). The nearest village to the Walks is Kirkoswald, about 2 miles (3 km) away. St Oswald's church stands in a hollow and over a well worshipped by pre-Christians. The bell tower was built on a hill nearby in an attempt to solve the problem of the sound of the bells carrying.

❿ PENRITH

One of the features of this border town is the ruined castle which stands in the public park. The small Penrith Museum (Middlegate), formerly a school (c 1670), provides a history of the area for visitors. (Open Easter–Oct daily; Nov–Mar, Mon–Sat). The steam museum (Castlegate) has displays of working engines and traction engines, a blacksmith's forge and a restored Victorian cottage. (Open Easter then Spring Bank Hol–Sept, Mon–Fri. Closed Sat (except Bank Hols) and Sun ♿ ⛴) Penrith Beacon (937 ft/288 m) is a great viewpoint.

One mile south of Penrith are two prehistoric monuments which provide evidence of the area's importance as a religious centre in years past. Arthur's Round Table is a henge (a bank with a ditch on the *inside*). Mayburgh Earthwork is a bank of cobbles rising to 15 feet (4.6 m) and surrounding a one and a half acre area. Within this ring there's one 9-foot (2.75 m) standing stone (the last stone in a circle of stones). (♿ to Arthur's Round Table) ☎ 0768 67466

⓫ SHAP

The ruined abbey hidden in a valley to the west of Shap was originally founded in 1199. The ground plan is quite obvious from what remains, and the tower (c 1500) survives well. (♿) Just south-east is the hamlet of Keld, where a small and very plain chapel of the 1400s (now belonging to the National Trust) speaks volumes about how poor and basic life was in the area.

⓬ WEATHERIGGS POTTERY

The pottery has been working since 1855 and has a museum, old machinery and demonstrations in pottery-making and weaving. (Open daily ♿. Phone 0768 62946)

43

South-West Lakeland

Preceding page: **Wastwater**

Wasdale Head

Muncaster Castle

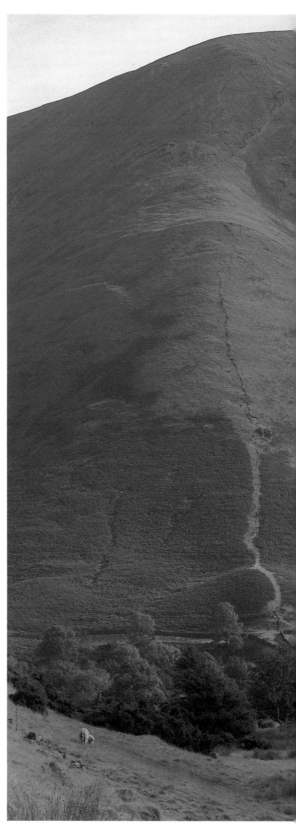

Wasdale Head Inn

This region is a mixture of natural scenic beauty and manmade landmarks. At one extreme there's Wastwater, one of the deepest and wildest lakes in England, and at the other, Sellafield – probably the most controversial industrial plant in the country. The varied scenery ranges from high volcanic crags, through granite dales to seaside sand-dunes. Settlements range from tiny, isolated sheep-farming hamlets to sleepy coastal villages. It's a surprising and largely undiscovered area.

Evidence of the area's industrial past is everywhere. The earliest miners in the region were the Romans, who produced smelted iron in Eskdale. Later, in the 1300s, the monks turned their hands to it, very successfully too. Hodbarrow used to be the world's largest iron-ore mine. The blood-red ore haemetite was discovered here in 1843 and by the 1860s 265 men were at work underground.

Woodland by Wastwater

Twenty years later, production was running at over 340,000 tons per annum. Millom was built around 1865 to house the miners and their families. Great barriers were also put up to keep the sea out of the workings and to help the men mine under the sea itself. One of these barriers is over a mile long.

Farther up the coast the Ravenglass and Eskdale railway was built to serve the Nab Gill mines at Boot. This mine was much less successful than Hodbarrow and in 1912 it was flooded out. The 3-foot (90 cm) industrial gauge was then changed to the present 15-inch (37.5 cm) gauge to fit Mr Bassett-Lowke's model trains, which were tested here. The trains still worked, carrying granite from

Irton Cross, St Paul's churchyard

Murthwaite; some of this went into the concrete for London's Waterloo Bridge.

Watermills were built to provide the power for forging, fulling cloth, wood turning and, of course, grinding corn. It's not surprising that there are so many mills to visit in the district today.

Sellafield is one of the world's largest nuclear power plants. Originally called Windscale, the plant started up in 1951 to make plutonium for nuclear bombs. In 1956 the world's first industrial reactor was built here. Today Sellafield is the world's largest nuclear reprocessing plant and, in 1988, the area's most visited tourist attraction, more popular even than Beatrix Potter's home.

Wastwater (58 ft/18 m below sea-level) is a product of the Ice Age when glaciers from the fells scooped out the valley and left in their place a cold, forbidding lake. This was originally filled with melted ice held in by a dam of debris that the glacier had deposited in the valley. The glacier couldn't escape from the valley and so pushed downwards, creating England's deepest lake.

Egremont Castle

Viking cross, Gosforth churchyard

Looking across Wastwater to Great Gable

Also in the valley of Wasdale are Scafell Pike, England's highest mountain; England's greatest liar, publican Will Ritson; and England's smallest church. The last claim is hotly disputed, but is valid if you work it out as cubic capacity for a used building.

Fell running is still a very popular sport among the locals and has produced some great Lakeland characters as well as remarkable achievements. One of the greatest of them all was the Lakeland guide Robert Graham. In 1932 Graham had set off from Keswick with the aim of running across the Lakeland peaks. He traversed nearly all of them in just under 23 hours 30 minutes. This was some performance and set a new record. The best known of recent fell runners is sheep farmer Joss Naylor, who is known locally as 'the flying shepherd'. Joss has traversed 72 Lakeland peaks (all above 2000 ft/610 m) in a time of 23 hours 11 minutes. This has involved running about 108 miles (173 km) and climbing c 40,000 feet (12,200 m). In other words he's climbed 10,972 feet 49

Shoreline, Wastwater

Evening, Wastwater

Sellafield nuclear plant

Bridge Inn, Santon

Ravenglass Station

(3352 m) higher than Everest. What's even more amazing is that Joss has had a bad back since the age of nine, and in recent years has had two discs removed. Surprising though it may seem, the fell running actually helps rather than aggravates this weakness. Joss was awarded the MBE in 1976.

Many of the district's place names owe their origins to the several different groups of invaders who settled here at various times over the centuries. After the Romans left Cumbria the Celts controlled the region, which they called 'Cymru' (meaning 'the people' or 'us'). Penrith is a Celtic name. The Celts were conquered by the Christian Anglians from across the Pennines. These people seem to have settled in the area's fertile lowlands and are thought to be responsible for the -ton ending in placenames. South-west of Wastwater there's a village called Irton, complete with an Anglian cross in the churchyard.

The words 'beck' (stream), 'gill' (ravine) and 'pike' (pointed hilltop) are Norse (northern Viking). The Norsemen roamed far and wide through the region. Norse words and place-names crop up all over and are more prevalent here than in any other area of Britain. The tangible evidence of the Viking presence, such as the Gosforth cross or the possible thing mound or parliament hill at Langdale, can seem so strange as to make it difficult for us to grasp the true extent of the Norsemen's influence. It's only when you start looking at the language and traditions of Cumbria that you realize how much of their culture the Norsemen left behind.

51

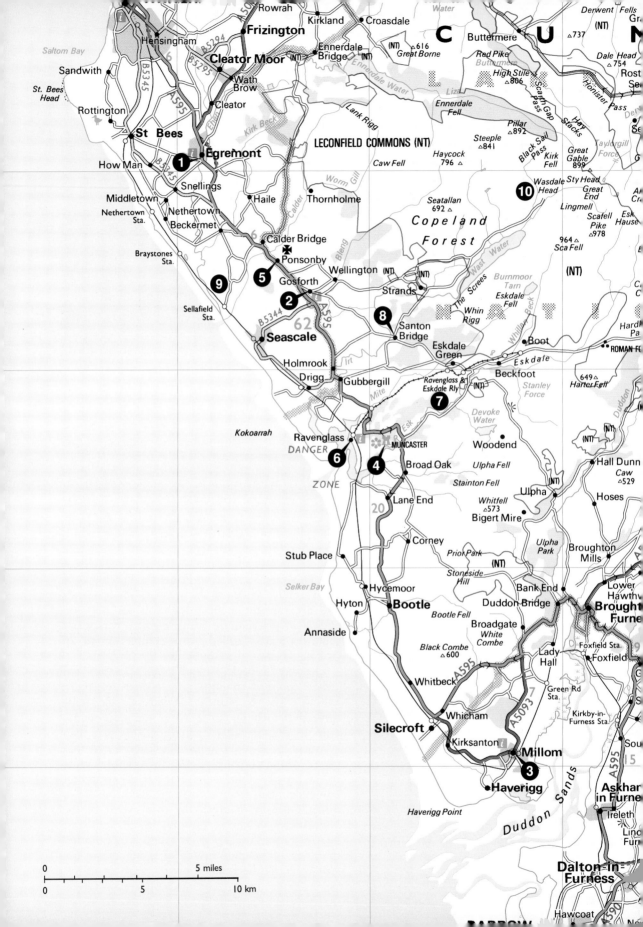

❶ EGREMONT

The main claim to fame of this small market town is the annual crab apple celebration, held in September since 1267. At noon a cartful of crab apples is thrown to the crowd followed by track and field events and hound trailing. In the the evening there's a competition for making the ugliest face within the frame of a horse collar; called 'gurning through a braffin'. There's a pipe-smoking contest and a 30-foot (9 m) greasy pole to climb for the prize of a leg of lamb.

The more serious side of local life can be savoured in the 18th-century Lowes Court Gallery, which specializes in showing the works of local artists. (Open all year, Mon–Sat; closed Wed afternoon. Phone 0946 820693) In the town's public park you'll find a 12th-century (c 1140) pink sandstone castle.

❷ GOSFORTH

In the churchyard there is a beautifully preserved 14-foot (4 m) high Viking cross dating to c 900 AD. The slender column is carved with myths of the Norse gods and one image of the crucified Christ. A similar carved cross can be seen in the churchyard at Irton, south-east of Gosforth.

❸ MILLOM

The town of Millom overlooks the Duddon Estuary. The Folk Museum (St George's Road) has a display of the life and work of the Lakeland poet Norman Nicholson and reconstructions of a Victorian miner's kitchen and of the local iron ore mine. (Open Easter and Spring Bank Hol weeks then Whitsun–mid Sept, Mon–Sat and Sun afternoon &) The site of the mine is now part of the RSPB's Hodbarrow Nature Reserve. A 3-mile (5 km) public footpath runs round the lagoon, through the reserve and along the side of the sea wall. ⧉ 0229 772555

❹ MUNCASTER CASTLE

This has been the home of the Pennington family since the 1200s. The oldest part of the castle, the pele tower, dates to 1345 but much of what you see today is Victorian. Inside, there are fine examples of

16th- and 17th-century furniture, tapestries and porcelain. Look out for the painting of Tom Skelton, the 16th-century fool of the Pennington family and the man after whom the word 'Tomfoolery' was coined. Outside there are rhododendron and azalea gardens and wonderful views over the Esk Valley. You'll also find a menagerie of bears, a commando course, model trains and the British Owl Breeding and Release Station. (Open Good Fri–30 Sept, Tues–Mon and Sun afternoon & ⅋. Phone 0229 717203)

❺ PONSONBY FARM PARK

This open farm has seven varieties of sheep, six of pig and four of cattle. There are three walking trails across the farm as well as a farmyard to explore. The Farm Park also has a tearoom, picnic area, rabbit run, pets' corner and a children's play area. (Open Easter then May–Sept daily ⅋. Phone 0946 841426)

Nearby is the ruined Calder Abbey (c 1130); the site is on private land and can only be seen from a footpath.

❻ RAVENGLASS

This town was a naval base in Roman times. The 12-foot (3.6 m) high walls of the old bath-house, called Walls Castle, are all that remain from this period. Later Ravenglass became a centre for pearl fishing and smuggling. These activities ended when the harbour silted up, creating dunes that now form part of the Eskmeals nature reserve. (Open all year; occasionally closes for gunnery practice. Always arrange in advance to visit Drigg Dunes reserve. Phone 0298 23456) ⧉ 0229 717278

❼ RAVENGLASS AND ESKDALE RAILWAY

England's oldest narrow-gauge system was started in 1875. The present 15-inch (37.5 cm) gauge, the 'La'al Ratty', generally runs steam services on the 7-mile (11 km) long track up Eskdale. You can visit the railway's museum at Ravenglass station. Tearooms at both Ravenglass and Eskdale termini. (Open Mar–Oct daily;

Sat–Sun only in winter & ⅋ (Ravenglass) Phone 0229 717171)

Muncaster Mill, a 19th-century water-powered corn mill with working machinery, can be reached by taking the train from Ravenglass and getting off at a request stop one mile down the line. In addition to the mill itself, there's a pets' corner and picnic area. (Open Apr–Sept, Sun–Fri)

Eskdale Corn Mill, at Boot, is a water-powered mill with farming and milling exhibitions and a comfortable walk from the terminus at Eskdale. Refreshments are available and there's a car park. If you have time, visit St Catherine's Church at Boot for its attractive setting. (Open Apr–Oct, Sun–Fri and Bank Hol Sat)

Stanley Ghyll, also called Dalegarth Falls, is a waterfall with three cascades, the largest of which is 37 feet (11 m). It's one mile south of Eskdale terminus, along a National Park nature trail.

❽ SANTON BRIDGE INN

This inn hosts the annual greatest liar competition (15 November). The contest starts after a supper of tatie pot, which is a sort of lamb stew. Entrants must either be locals or foreigners and strictly amateur – politicians and lawyers aren't allowed to enter!

❾ SELLAFIELD

The exhibition centre shows videos, computer games and working models to explain the workings of the nuclear industry. There are also coach tours around the site. Refreshments. (Open daily & ⅋. Phone 0946 773439)

❿ WASDALE HEAD

This wild place is considered the cradle of British rock climbing, for it was here that Britain's first climbing association was set up. The rugged mountains above and behind the Wastwater have claimed the lives of several mountaineers; their graves can be seen in the tiny church of St Olaf.

The Wasdale Head Inn is famous for having had Will Ritson (1808–90), Britain's greatest liar, as its landlord. Photographs of the old rogue still hang in the inn.

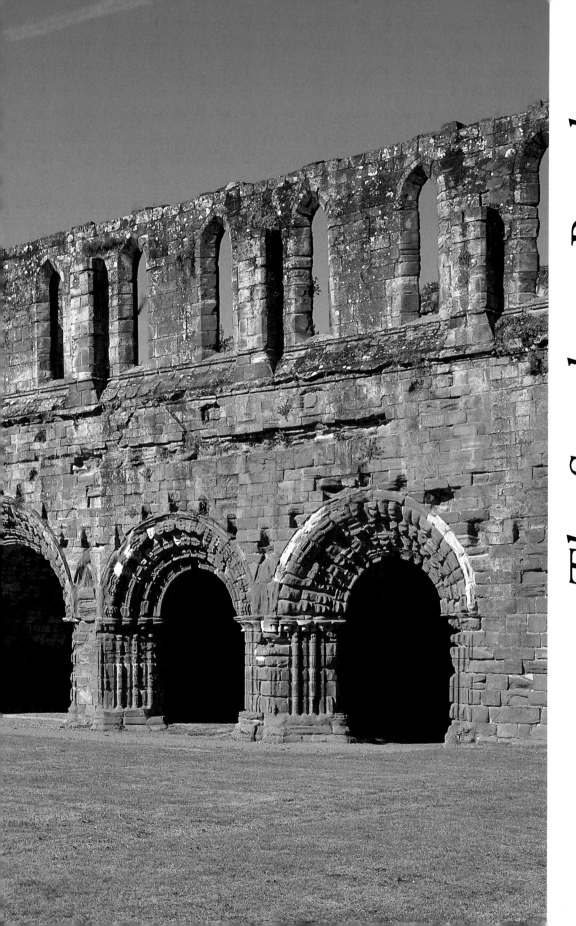

The Southern Reaches

Coniston Water

Roa Island

Preceding page: **Furness Abbey, Barrow**

At one end of this diverse area you'll find rugged mountain passes and few inhabitants, and at the other the heavily industrial Barrow-in-Furness with a population of over 60,000. Between these two extremes are bustling market towns and a soft, sandy coastline. Among the many sites are monasteries and mineshafts, and fells, fortresses and nature reserves.

The Romans set up 20 forts in this area between 98 and 138 AD but left little evidence of their occupation and in some places stayed only a comparatively short time. The fort in Hardknott Pass, for example, was probably abandoned altogether after 197 AD. It stands halfway between the Roman forts at Ambleside and Ravenglass, in a most inhospitable part of the region. The Roman soldiers posted here must have wondered which of their gods they'd offended. The road built by the Romans to connect all three forts continued to Watercrook, near Kendal and, from there, joined the main road to Carlisle and Lowbarrow bridge, south of Tebay. An alternative route from

Ship Inn, Piel Island

Ulverston Sands

Cockley Beck Fell

Slate footpath sign

Ambleside leads to another fort at Brougham, near Penrith. This route was, and still is, quite spectacular. Called High Street, it runs along the ridge of mountains south of Ullswater. Brougham fort is fairly unusual among the Roman forts of central Lakeland in that there seems to have been a large civilian township (vicus) outside its walls.

If you're a good walker or climber the best place to start exploring the area is, quite literally, at the top, round Scafell Pike, England's highest mountain (3210 ft/978 m); this now belongs to the

Rail viaduct across Morecambe Bay

Brantwood

Drinking fountain, Dalton-in-Furness

Piel Castle, Piel Island

National Trust and was given in memory of the dead of World War I. An extraordinary character called Alfred Wainwright got to know Lakeland in precisely this way over forty years ago. Wainwright's lifelong love affair with the Lake District began when he holidayed there as a young man. Over ten years later he took a drop in salary and moved to Kendal in order to be nearer his beloved fells. In 1952 he decided to climb and record all the Lakeland fells and mountains. With the precision you'd expect of a man who was now Kendal's borough treasurer, Wainwright calculated that it would take him 13 years to complete his task – and it did. The results of his labours run into seven volumes, entitled *The Pictorial Guide to the Lakeland Fells*, and are invaluable to the serious walker or climber. The books are facsimiles of Wainwright's original manuscripts, handwritten and with his own pen and ink drawings as illustrations. All proceeds from the book are donated to Animal Rescue Cumbria, a charity whick looks after stray dogs and cats. Wainwright's efforts were recognized with the award of an MBE. If you are interested in knowing more about his life, the museum at Brantwood has a small, permanent display devoted to him which includes his drawings, pipe and, predictably, boots and socks as exhibits.

If you want to experience the joys of fell walking, make sure that you go well prepared. Recommended items include light boots that support the ankles and have non-slip soles, a detailed map (preferably 1:25,000 scale) and a rucksack. The sack should contain vital items such as a torch, compass, whistle and emergency rations, in addition to extra clothing in case the weather worsens; take a sweater, socks and a hat as it can get very cold up there. Make sure you have windproof and waterproof clothing as well, including leggings. A successful expedition depends on good planning. Don't try to cover too many miles too quickly: two miles an hour is about right, and add an hour for every 1000 feet (305 m) you climb. Check out the weather in advance by ringing 09662 5151 for a taped forecast. Plan, too, an alternative route, just in case mother nature springs a nasty and unexpected surprise. Lastly, let someone know where you are going and when you expect to return.

The great 19th-century art critic and art historian, John Ruskin was, like Alfred Wainwright, an 'outsider' who felt a strong

59

View from Broughton Fell

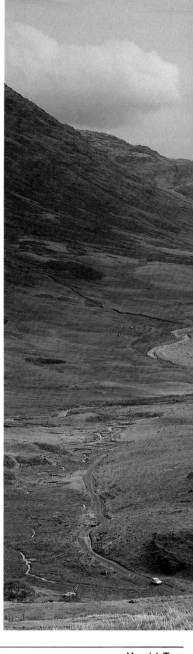

Urswick Tarn

affinity with Lakeland early in life. In Ruskin's case this was very early indeed; his first childhood memory was of walking with his nurse on Friar's Crag at Derwentwater, and at the age of five he had his first view of Coniston Water. Ruskin did not become a resident of Lakeland until 1871, some 47 years after his first visit, when he bought a house called Brantwood. The house stands at the edge of Coniston Water and is said to be the most beautifully situated in the whole of the Lake District. Ruskin must have been convinced of this claim because he happily paid £1500 without

Sir John Barrow memorial, Ulverston

Wrynose Bottom

Climbers at Hoad Hill, Ulverston

seeing the property. Visitors still marvel at the impressive setting and the wonderful lake and mountain views. Brantwood was Ruskin's base until he died, in 1900.

Although primarily remembered today for his influence in the field of art, Ruskin was also a tireless advocate of social justice and a vociferous critic of the adverse effects of industrialization; many of the 250 books written by him reflect these concerns. Ruskin wanted to help make the world a better place and art had a role in this. His defence of both Turner and the pre-Raphaelite Brother-

hood of artists in the face of widespread hostility to their work was based on an admiration of their purity of purpose as much as an appreciation of their respective techniques. Watercolours by Turner used to be a feature of Ruskin's bedroom at Brantwood and he owned several paintings by the pre-Raphaelites Burne-Jones and Holman-Hunt.

Ruskin himself was an accomplished water-colourist and a major expansion is underway at Brantwood to cope with the 'bringing home' of his many paintings and drawings.

❶ BARDSEA

The coastal country park here has large woodland areas with wonderful views over Morecambe Bay. (Open at all times &) There's another fine viewpoint just west of the park, at Birkrigg Common. Margaret Fox, the mother of Quakerism, is buried here, in Sunbrick Burial Ground. Nearby is the Gothic Conishead Priory (1821), now a Tibetan Buddhist centre. The woodland trail across Priory land gives some idea of the beauty of this 70-acre estate. Coffee shop. (House open Easter–Sept, Sat–Sun and Bank Hols. Phone 0229 54029) About 3 miles (5 km) south-west of the Priory is Gleaston's working watermill, which has craft workshops and a restaurant. (Open Easter–Sept, Tues–Sun. Phone 0229 869244)

❷ BARROW-IN-FURNESS

The museum (Ramsden Square) in this shipbuilding town covers all aspects of the town's history. (Open Mon and Wed–Sat; closed Thurs afternoon) North of the town are the red sandstone remains of Furness Abbey, founded in 1127. (Museum and ruins open Apr–Oct daily; Nov–Mar, Tues–Sat and Sun afternoon) South of Barrow is Piel Castle, a 14th-century defensive tower. The ferry service runs from here to Roa island which, together with Foulney and Walney, is famous for its wildlife. There's a nature trail at Westfield, north of Roa. One of Europe's largest gulleries lies the other side of Walney channel. (South Walney gullery and nature reserve open Tues–Sun and Bank Hols) ☎ 0229 870156

❸ BRANTWOOD

There's lots for the visitor to see here. Inside the house is a video film of John Ruskin's life and an exhibition of his paintings and some personal possessions. There's also a room devoted to Alfred Wainwright, a tea room, craft gallery and bookshop. Outside there's a nature trail, a garden and a pier for the steam yacht *Gondola*. (Open mid Mar–mid Nov daily. Rest of the year, Wed–Sun & 05394 41396)

❹ BROUGHTON-IN-FURNESS

The square in this small, friendly 18th-century market town has an obelisk at its centre and fish slabs and stocks nearby.

❺ CONISTON

This dour village used to be famous for its copper; 900 miners worked here in the 19th century. The National Trust owns the 17th-century Old Hall, which they hope to open to the public soon. In the churchyard is a Celtic cross memorial to John Ruskin. The Ruskin museum (Yewdale Road) covers local history, including the story of the world speed record attempts on Coniston Water. (Open Easter–Oct daily) ☎ 05394 41533

❻ CONISTON WATER

The Campbells' association with Coniston Water began in 1939 when the first *Bluebird* powerboat, driven by Malcolm Campbell, set a new world speed record of 141.74 mph (226.8 km/h) but which unfortunately ended tragically on 4 January 1967 with Donald Campbell's fatal crash in *Bluebird* during another record attempt. These days a totally different kind of vessel plies the waters, the steam yacht *Gondola* (1859). You can now glide across the lake in fully restored Victorian splendour, thanks to the National Trust. (Regular sailings Apr–early Nov. Piers at Coniston, Brantwood and Park-a-Moor) Alternatively, you can paddle your own canoe or captain your own rowing boat, sailing dinghy or motor boat by hiring one from the National Park's boating centre at Coniston.

❼ DALTON-IN-FURNESS

The castle here is really only a tower, built in the 1300s by the monks of Furness Abbey. (Open Apr–late Sept daily; Sat afternoons only. Phone 05394 33883) George Romney (1734–1802), the famous portrait painter, was born in the town and, after a lifetime spent away from it, is buried here.

❽ HARDKNOTT AND WRYNOSE PASSES

With 1:3 gradients en route and sheer drops off route, this place isn't for the faint hearted. To make matters worse, the road can get very crowded in summer. At the summit of Wrynose Pass (1281 ft/391 m) you'll find the Three Shires Stone to mark the point where, until 1974, Lancashire, Westmoreland and Cumberland met. Now, whichever way you turn, it's Cumbria. Hardknott rises higher than Wrynose, to 1291 feet (394 m). Near the top is the Roman fort of Mediobogdum, built (c 130 AD) to house a garrison of 500 or so infantry. The walls, with corner towers and gates on each side, are still standing, as are the foundations of the HQ, the granary, the commander's house and the bathhouse. (Open all year daily)

❾ ULVERSTON

The landmark at Ulverston is a 100-foot (30.5 m) tall 'lighthouse' on top of Hoad Hill, a memorial to local lad Sir John Barrow (1764–1848), who was secretary to the Admiralty for 40 years. The town has a wide variety of attractions. Furness Galleries (Theatre Street) is renowned for dolls' houses and furniture hand-made on the premises, which also houses an exhibition area, craft shop and coffee shop. (Open Mon–Sat &) Cumbria Crystal (Lightburn Road) runs an excellent factory tour which includes demonstrations of full lead crystal being blown, cut and polished. (Open Mon–Fri &) The Laurel and Hardy museum (Stan Laurel was born here in 1890) in Upper Brook Street has mementoes, photographs and films of the great comic duo. (Open Mon, Tues and Thurs–Sat)

Just outside Ulverston, on the Barrow road, stands Swarthmoor Hall (1586), the first Quaker centre. The Hall was the home of Judge Thomas Fell and his wife Margaret in the 17th century. They befriended George Fox, the leader of the Quakers, from 1652 onwards. Eleven years after Judge Fell's death, in 1658, Fox and Margaret married. Today the house is still owned by the Society of Friends and is open to visitors. (Open mid Mar–mid Oct, Mon–Wed and Sat) ☎ 0229 57120

Sheep-Farming in Lakeland

The four-hourly feed (EJF)

Tending ewes in winter, Kirkstone Pass (EJF)

Farmer shearing with hand clippers (EJF)

Inspecting tups at market (EJF)

Preceding page: Gathering sheep at Watendlath (EJF)

Herdwick tups (EJF)

Yan, Tyan, Tethera, Methera, Pimp, Sethera, Lethera, Hovera, Dovera, Dick – your eyelids should be drooping by now because you've been counting sheep Borrowdale style; Yan is one and Dick is ten.

Cumbria is home to 10 per cent of the sheep in England. The commonest breed in Lakeland nowadays is the dark-faced, grey-muzzled Swaledale, which has several advantages over the most traditional breed, the thick set, white-faced Herdwick. Swaledales breed younger, produce better quality wool and have more milk. Herdwicks produce more wool but of a rougher texture;

Returning ewes to the fell, Langdale

theirs is generally used for carpets whereas the soft Swaledale wool is of the right quality for sweaters. Herdwicks are tougher customers all round, able to withstand harsh conditions – such as surviving for two weeks in a snowdrift – and nimble enough to jump over a 4-foot wall. Sheep-farmers admire the physical prowess of the hardy Herdwick but prefer the economic edge of the Swaledale.

The sheep-farmer's year typically begins in November when the tups (or rams) are run with the ewes on the better land lower down. A tup is expected to service about 60 ewes and gets extra feed for extra work (hence the expression 'getting your oats'). The ewes are then moved to higher land, ideally onto the fellside. It's vital that the ewes have been well fed before they are moved. They can lose up to 20 per cent of their bodyweight and an undernourished ewe may even re-absorb her foetus in an attempt to make up the nutritional shortfall. The farmer gives his ewes extra feed during the last weeks of pregnancy to help them though this vital period.

In April the ewes are gradually rounded up on the high ground. Fell dogs (sheepdogs that can work alone and a long way from the shepherd) are used for this task. Lambing takes place on the lower ground. A different kind of sheepdog is needed to herd the ewes at this time. The dogs mustn't bark or frighten the nervous animals but do their job quietly and unobtrusively. Ideally, lambing will be completed in May and the flock taken back to the fellside. This allows the farmer to get a crop of hay for feed from his lower land. The sheep are brought back down again in July for shearing and dipping, and then it's back up again to the higher land until October when the sheep sales start. Young males and 4- or 5-year-old Swaledale ewes may be sold to farms in the lowlands, the males for fattening for meat and the ewes for interbreeding with lowland rams. The ewes and rams that are kept back by the sheep-farmers will begin the process all over again come November.

Sheep-farming in Lakeland is a hard way of earning a living. The land in the region is generally low grade and, on the fells, it's winter for ten months of the year. Farmers receive very little for their wool and the subsidies for stock and grants for improvements, on which they rely, are decreasing. The drop in the value of agricultural land and stock is a stark reflection of the problems they face. And yet although many of these farmers live on the economic margin, they are in many ways at the centre of the constant struggle to keep Lakeland looking its best. It is they who perform the tricky and time-consuming task of maintaining the traditional drystone walls, and who discourage the relentless march of that poisonous weed bracken, which advances at the rate of one yard per year over the best soil unless checked.

There are several sheep events held annually in Lakeland. The most popular are the Wasdale Show in October and the sheepdog trials at Rydal and Patterdale in August.

West Windermere

Wooden sculpture, Grizedale Forest Park

Elterwater

A corner of Hawkshead

Hill Top Farm, near Sawrey

70   *Preceding page:* **Grizedale Forest**

The Hawkshead area is like a self-contained island, flanked by Coniston Water to the west and Windermere to the east. It's topped by the volcanic crags and waterfalls around Elterwater in the north, and it's tailed by the River Leven's estuary in the south. Almost all the region's rock is of the soft, sedimentary, south Lakeland type, which gives broad valleys, low hills and gentle slopes. This means there's more farmland, hamlets and villages than natural dramatic features, but it's a very beautiful area nonetheless.

The area's woodland was also one of its economic mainstays; there are records of the industry dating back to 1430 and only eventually fading out about 100 years ago. The woodland industry here was called coppicing. Each tree trunk was cut down so as to produce long thin poles from the shoots. The process gave about 15 poles per tree every 15 years. Many of the poles

Hawkshead Grammar School

were made into charcoal locally on circular platforms called pitsteads. The charcoal was then used to fire the bloomeries that made iron. (Bloomery sites are easy to find – just look for the slag heaps.) More sophisticated blast furnaces were eventually introduced but charcoal held its place in the iron industry for a very long time; at Ealing Hearth near Backbarrow they were still using it in 1936.

The charcoal had other uses. It's a basic ingredient of gunpowder, so this too was made in the district. Naturally, such factories were built in isolated areas because of the danger of accidents; in 1863 an explosion at the Low Wood factory killed six and was heard as far away as Keswick. Once made, the powder was stored in barrels. About 100 years ago a quarter of a million barrels were needed every year for the gunpowder alone.

Stott Park Bobbin Mill

71

Lakeside & Haverthwaite Railway engine

Tarn Hows

In addition to providing the wood for the barrels, the coppiced woodland also supplied the wood for bobbins, the reels then used for winding cotton in factories. One large mill could use ten million bobbins and 10 per cent of these needed replacing every week. Lakeland wood also went into making carts, clogs, pick-axe handles and toggles for Royal Navy duffle coats. Some of the oak poles were split into thin strips and then woven to make swill baskets. The bark of oak trees was also used, to make tannin for tanning leather; half a woodsman's income could come from this alone. It really was a case of 'there's gold to be made out of them thar woods'.

Charcoal burners crop up as 'colliers' in Arthur Ransome's book, *Swallows and Amazons*. Ransome claimed to be the youngest person ever to reach the top of Coniston Old Man – his father had carried him there when he was only a few weeks old, in 1884. The Ransome family generally spent their holidays on or around Coniston Water; Bethecar, near Nibthwaite, was a favourite base. Arthur attended a prep school at Windermere and decided at this time that he wanted to be a writer. Though his own family were opposed to the idea, he persisted and was given great encouragement by the brilliant Collingwoods, the owners of the original *Swallow*. Ransome's writing was inter-

Haverthwaite Station

Grizedale Forest Park

Parachute water tank, Haverthwaite Station

rupted by World War I and the Russian Revolution, the events of which he covered as a reporter. When he eventually managed to get back to the Lakes, in 1925, he bought a house at Low Ludderburn, near Windermere, and settled down to his chosen career. *Swallows and Amazons* was published in 1930. Appropriately, *Esperance* (Captain Flint's houseboat in the book) can be found at the Windermere Steamboat museum today. Ransome had a series of Lakeland homes from 1925 until his death in 1967. His last was Hill Top at Haverthwaite. The writer is buried at Rusland and you can see a replica of his writing room at Kendal.

Beatrix Potter is another famous writer with a strong Lakeland connection. At Hill Top, near Sawrey, you can see the 'new room' where she did much of her work. The whole house is exactly as Beatrix Potter knew it. She bought Hill Top in 1905 with the proceeds from her first book, *The Tale of Peter Rabbit*, which she had originally published herself after seven publishers turned it down. The book had started as a letter to a little boy called Noel, the son of a former governess, in 1893. In the letter Beatrix confided that she hadn't an idea what to write to him about so she'd tell him a story with pictures instead. The inspiration for the story had come to Beatrix many years 73

Tarn Hows

Anne Tyson's cottage, Hawkshead

A village inn

View across Tarn Hows

earlier, in the 1880s when as a girl of 16 she had first visited the Lakes with her parents and stayed at Wray Castle which they had rented for the duration of the holiday. And so began Beatrix's love affair with the region and the stimulus which found expression in her animal characters and their adventures. Beatrix's suffocatingly formal parents did not encourage her to write, and the only support she received was from the local vicar and founder of the National Trust, Hardwicke

Wray Castle

Rawnsley. The purchase of Hill Top was a long-overdue bid for independence. Beatrix wrote 13 books over a period of eight years in the few weeks each year she could snatch away from her demanding parents and spend at the house. During this time she met William Heelis, a local Hawkshead solicitor, who helped her buy Castle Farm in 1909. The couple married in 1913, much to the displeasure of her parents who thought she'd married beneath her. Castle Farm now became Beatrix's main home, with Hill Top kept on as her private museum. From this point on, Beatrix more or less stopped writing and put her energies into new interests. Breeding Herdwick sheep and the conservation of the Lakeland countryside became her passions. When she died in 1943, aged 77, she left 15 farms and over 4000 acres to the National Trust. However, it's because of her books that people visit Hill Top in their droves. There's a special magic in recognizing Tom Kitten's stamping ground or being able to see the very doll's house that 'the two bad mice' wrecked so effectively.

❶ ELTERWATER

The name 'Elterwater' literally means swan lake in Norse. The lake itself is the smallest in Lakeland. To its north is the site of an old gunpowder works, now a time-share property with an excellent sports centre which you can use if you buy a day ticket. (The Langdale Country Club is open daily. Phone 09667 391 ♿)

Also to the north is Fibrecrafts of Barnhowe, a firm specializing in handspinning, weaving and dyeing supplies. Half-day courses are held on handspinning. (Open Easter–Nov daily; closed Sun afternoon ♿. Phone 09667 346)

To the south of Elterwater are the villages of Skelwith Bridge and Colwith, noted for their waterfalls.

❷ GRAYTHWAITE HALL GARDENS

This place is a must for flower enthusiasts: 7 acres of rhododendrons, azaleas and flowering shrubs set in grounds landscaped by Thomas Mawson between 1888 and 1890. (Open Apr–Jun daily)

❸ GRIZEDALE FOREST PARK

Here you'll find displays on the forest and its wildlife through the ages. There are computers, a shop, wildlife playground, orienteering trails, seven waymarked walks, hides where you can watch wildlife and a collection of modern sculpture. (Centre open Apr–Oct and late Dec daily ♿ ⛴. Forest and trails open all year. Phone 0229 860373)

❹ HAWKSHEAD

This picturesque village of white-washed cottages and meandering cobbled streets is very popular. There's a large car park just outside the village. The grammar school (founded in 1588 and housed in a building of 1675) was attended by William Wordsworth between 1779 and 1787. You can see the desk on which he carved his name. (Open Easter–Oct daily) William boarded with Anne Tyson. Her house in the village is marked with a plaque, although it is uncertain whether William lodged at this particular house. The Beatrix Potter Gallery (Main Street) has on dis-

play around 150 of the writer's illustrations. It used to be the office of Beatrix's husband, William Heelis, and is virtually unchanged since his time. (Open Apr–early Nov, Mon–Fri) There are some lovely views to be had from the church, St Michael's, which dates from Tudor times.

About half a mile north of the village is Hawkshead Courthouse, dating from the 1400s. It was part of Hawkshead Hall and is all that is left of the manorial buildings once owned by the monks of Furness Abbey. (Open Apr–early Nov daily; key obtainable from National Trust shop at Hawkshead) If you head south out of Hawkshead village, you'll come to Esthwaite Water, a private lake. The trout farm on the west side of the lake keeps the waters well stocked for anglers. Rainbow trout grow to almost 13 lb (6 kg)! There's an attractive picnic area and boats can be hired at the southern end of the lake. (Open daily) ☎ 09666 525

❺ HILL TOP

This small 17th-century house near Sawrey was the first of several homes owned by Beatrix Potter. While living at Hill Top she wrote many of her best-loved books and introduced characters such as Tom Kitten, Samuel Whiskers and Jemimah Puddleduck. Today the house is a museum devoted to every aspect of the life and work of its former owner and is exactly as she knew it, right down to the furniture and china. Hill Top is very popular; so much so that the National Trust has had to stop publicizing it. (Open Apr–early Nov, Mon–Wed and Sat–Sun ⛴. Phone 09666 269) Nearby, close to Far Sawrey, is the ferry landing. From here a 6-mile (9 km) way-marked (with white posts) path leads you up Claife Heights and on to Hawkshead. If the whole route sounds too strenuous, just do the first half-mile – you'll be rewarded with magnificent views.

❻ LAKESIDE & HAVERTHWAITE RAILWAY

The steam trains of this railway connect with the steamers on Lake

Windermere. The trip takes 18 minutes one way. (Trains run daily over Easter then early May–early Oct ♿ ⛴. The collection of locomotives at Haverthwaite is open daily. Phone 05395 31594)

Sights en route include: At Lakeside, the Campbell Legend Exhibition on board the lake cruiser *Swift*. This houses replicas of the *Bluebird* car of 1935 and the *Bluebird* hydroplane of 1967. (Open Easter Sun–late Oct daily ⛴. Phone 05395 58509)

At Low Wood, near Haverthwaite, the old gunpowder works are occupied by craftsmen. Art crystal is housed in the Clock Tower building, where you can see demonstrations of glass engraving. (Open Tues–Sun)

❼ RUSLAND HALL

Built in 1720 and with gardens landscaped by 'Capability' Brown, this is now a high-class hotel. The future of the gardens is uncertain. (Phone 0229 860276) The writer Arthur Ransome is buried in Rusland churchyard.

❽ STOTT PARK BOBBIN MILL

Don't be put off by the rather dull sounding name. This working factory, built in 1835, is a genuine slice of the past, preserved in all its glory by English Heritage. (Open Apr–Oct daily ♿ ⛴. Phone 0448 31087)

❾ TARN HOWS

Lakeland connoisseurs shun this place precisely because it is a great favourite of so many other people. The views are super but you'll have to arrive early to avoid the crush.

❿ WRAY CASTLE

This place, in the village of Low Wray, looks like a Hollywood film set but is, in fact, a Victorian folly (built 1840–7). It used to be the home of a Liverpool surgeon and is now a college for marine engineers. (The grounds are open to the public; the house by arrangement only Jul–Aug)

Just south of High Wray is Latterbarrow, an excellent and very accessible viewpoint (803 ft/ 245 m); approach via the footpath from the west.

South-East Lakeland

Brockhole National Park Centre

Waterhead, Windermere

The shores of Windermere and the valley of the River Kent become very crowded in summer so you may prefer to explore the hills between the two. The minor roads and small farming settlements lend a quiet and very appealing charm to this south-east corner of Lakeland.

The area is dominated by Kendal, which has many more attractions than any other town in the Lake District. Often called the gateway to the Lakes, Kendal is still involved in manufacturing.

Items ranging from snuff to K's shoes (the K standing for Kendal) are made here. The town is the home of Kendal Mint Cake, a mixture of a little mint essence, some glucose and lots of sugar. This concoction has been carried on many an expedition and has even been eaten on top of Mount Everest.

Kendal has been famous for its cloth for many centuries; the town's motto 'Pannus mihi Panis' ('cloth is my bread') reflects this. In the Middle

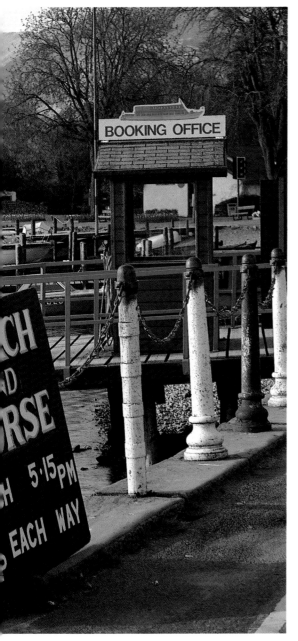

Lake Windermere

The Mason's Arms, Cartmel Fell

Ages there was a type of cloth called Kendal Green which was heavy, warm, waterproof and often dyed green, hence the name. In Shakespeare's plays, Kendal Green seems either to have been worn almost exclusively by 'knaves' or it turns up in 'threadbare' condition. Luxury cloth was also made in Kendal. In 1543 King Henry VIII was so impressed by the gift of a coat of Kendal cloth that he ordered another and started a fashion for it at court. The present was given by local resident Catherine Parr, who was born at Kendal Castle in 1512. Later she became his sixth wife and fortunately managed to bury him before he could either divorce or execute her. Henry was her third husband. Catherine married her love, Sir Thomas Seymour, in 1547 but sadly died a year later shortly after giving birth to their first child. The town proudly preserves Catherine's own tiny, handwritten prayerbook; it's only $2\frac{1}{3}$ in × $1\frac{1}{2}$ in (6 cm × 4 cm). If you'd like to see it, enquire at the

81

Holy Trinity parish church, Kendal

River Kent, Kendal

Kendal

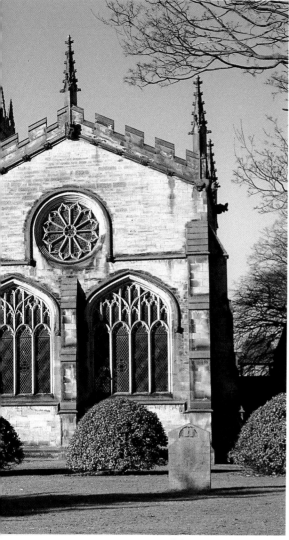

Ruins on Castle Hill, Kendal

Tourist Information Centre in The Town Hall, where it's kept.

The region produces both dairy cattle (generally Friesians) and beef cattle (mainly Friesian cows crossed with foreign bulls such as Simmentals or Limousins). The advantage of cattle is that they help improve hill land by eating coarse grass that sheep won't touch. The disadvantages are that they put on less weight in comparison to sheep – particularly on poorer grass – and need a good supply of feed in winter when they're housed. In 1986 sheep outnumbered cattle by nearly 9:1 in

Waterside, Kendal

the National Park, although cattle remain a vital part of the farming industry.

Just 2 miles (3 km) south of Kendal is a railway junction called Oxenholme. From here a single line branches off the Euston–Glasgow mainline and potters gently on through the countryside via Kendal and Staveley to Windermere. It's difficult to credit that this humble little track used to carry the Lakes Express, a superb train connecting London with Lakeland. The nondescript two-carriage diesel units nowadays used by British Rail on this line look out of place in the 100-yard long platforms built at Windermere to accommodate the Express. When the idea of building the line was first mooted, Wordsworth was one of the many people in the area who bitterly opposed it. His main objection was that it would allow hordes of 'uneducated people' into *his* countryside. These philistines wouldn't appreciate what they saw and would only ruin it for the minority who could 83

Newby Bridge

Ennerdale Water

appreciate it. Despite a thunderous sonnet published in the *Morning Post* (beginning: 'Is there no nook of English ground secure from rash assault?'), Wordsworth lost. The line was built but stopped three-quarters of a mile short of the lakeside so as not to disturb the 'quality' dwelling in their villas. Later attempts to extend the line were quashed by the two R's – Rawnsley and Ruskin, representing the great and the good of Victorian England.

(Trains run almost hourly in the weekdays. Journey duration: about 25 minutes.)

Wordsworth also hated the indiscriminate planting of larch trees and the selfish positioning of brand new whitewashed houses just where they did maximum damage to the views. In many ways he's one of the early conservationists. In his *Guide to the Lakes* (a best-seller which, ironically, did much to encourage yet more visitors to flock to *his*

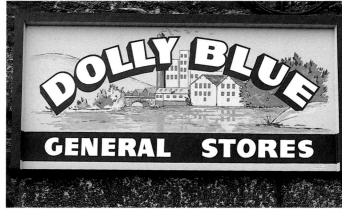

Shop sign, Backbarrow, Newby Bridge

Lakeland) Wordsworth came up with the idea that there ought to be some control system to stop the region being ruined. He went on to describe the district as 'a sort of national property, in which every man has a right and interest who has an eye to perceive and a heart to enjoy'. Nothing came of this idea until 1951 when the Lake District National Park, embracing 880 square miles (2279 sq km), was established. (By contrast, in the United States Yellowstone National Park was set up in 1876.)

Land ownership didn't change as a result of the creation of the National Park, but it did mean that special planning restrictions were introduced. A special body (called the Lake District Special Planning Board or the National Park Authority) was also set up to protect the region, keep it beautiful and help the public appreciate it.

❶ BOWNESS

The attractions of this lakeside town are appropriately watery. The Windermere Aquarium shows British fish, including many that are found in the Lakes. (Open Mar–Oct daily) The Windermere Steamboat Museum (Raynrigg Road) has two record-breakers on display: *Dolly* (c 1850), the oldest mechanically powered boat in the world; and *Esperance* (1869), the oldest boat on Lloyd's Register. Beatrix Potter's rowing boat is here, as is an elegant launch called *Branksome* which has a tea urn that can boil a gallon of water in ten seconds! The museum also operates steamboat cruises on the lake. (Open Easter–Oct daily &) ☎ 09662 2895

❷ BROCKHOLE

This is the National Park Centre. It bills itself as 'the Key to the Lakes' and aims to give the new visitor a thorough introduction to the area. There's an exhibition on Lakeland life here through the centuries, a sideshow on Beatrix Potter and superb audio-visual programme. The programme of special activities can range from dog obedience classes, through open air theatre to household cavalry displays. In the grounds (landscaped by Thomas Mawson) you'll find well-tended flowerbeds, putting and croquet lawns, and an adventure playground. There are also orienteering and nature trails to follow. Restaurant. (Open late Mar–Sept daily &. Phone 09662 6601)

❸ FELL FOOT COUNTRY PARK

All that remains of the Georgian house that used to stand here are its outbuildings. These have been converted by the National Trust into a shop, information centre and café. The 18 acres of land on the lakeshore also belong to the Trust. The place is worth visiting for the views alone. There are also fishing, bathing and picnic areas, and rowing boats for hire. (Park open all year daily. Amenities open Easter–end Oct daily &. Phone 05395 31273)

❹ GUMMERS HOWE

This fine viewpoint (1054 ft/324 m) is reached after a half-mile walk from the car park on the C road leading from the Fell Foot area.

❺ KENDAL

Once the county town of Westmorland, Kendal has a lot to offer, including a very large and fine parish church, the remains of two castles (both open at any time) and Castle Dairy (Wildman Street), parts of which date back to the 1300s. (Open Easter–Sept, Weds afternoons only) There are several museums here. Abbot Hall (Kirkland) is a Georgian house containing antique porcelain, glass, silver, furniture and paintings, as well as a fine collection of modern art. Part of the Abbot Hall complex houses the Museum of Lakeland Life, which vividly illustrates everyday life in the area with replicas of a Victorian street, farmhouse rooms, workshops and Arthur Ransome's study. Kendal Museum (Station Road) specializes in local history (including natural history) and has a display devoted to fell walker Arthur Wainwright. (All three museums are open Spring Bank Hol–Oct daily except Sun morning. Rest of year, daily except Sat and Sun mornings &) Kendal also has a lively Brewery Arts Centre (Highgate), with several restaurants. (Open Mon–Sat &) You can see Axminster carpets being made at Goodacre Carpets (Aynam Road). (Open mid Apr–mid Oct, Wed and Fri afternoons &) Kendal usually hosts The Westmorland County Show in mid September. The Kendal Gathering is a festival that starts on August Bank Holiday weekend and ends about three weeks later. The torchlight procession is one of the highlights of the festival and very popular. ☎ 0539 725758

❻ SCOUT SCAR

This viewpoint (813 ft/250 m) is easily reached from the car park in the quarry midway between Kendal and Underbarrow.

❼ SIZERGH CASTLE

The Strickland family have lived here for over 700 years. The pele tower (1340) is the largest in Cumbria. There's fine furniture and porcelain inside the house, including what are reputed to be the finest early Elizabethan woodcarvings in England. Outside there's the largest rock garden owned by the National Trust as well as rose, water and Dutch gardens. Tearoom. (Open Apr–Oct, Sun–Mon and Wed–Thurs &. Phone 05395 60070)

❽ STAVELEY

Formerly a centre of woodland industry, the town has as one of its main features the firm of Peter Hall & Son, specialists in cabinet making, antique furniture restoring, woodturning and traditional upholstering. You can watch the craftsmen at work and buy the result. (Open Mon–Fri &. Phone 0539 821633)

❾ WINDERMERE

This is the largest lake in England, at 10½ miles (17 km) long and about a mile wide at its broadest point. On Windermere's largest island (just opposite Bowness) is the first round house built in England. Belle Isle house, built in 1774, was the home of the Curwens from 1781. (Not open)

There are three ways to cross the lake. A car ferry sails from Bowness Nab to Far Sawrey about every 20 minutes. (Runs every day except Christmas and Boxing Days.) The Bowness Bay Boating Company operates passenger services between Bowness and Ambleside; some ferries stop at Brockhole in the summer, others do a circular cruise. (Open daily except Christmas Day. One launch is wheelchair accessible.) The Windermere Iron Steamboat Company, based at Newby Bridge, sails between Lakeside, Bowness and Ambleside; the full one-way trip takes about 1 hour and 20 minutes. (Runs Good Friday–early Nov &)

❿ WINDERMERE TOWN

Windermere is really an expanded hamlet called Birthwaite and is situated one mile from the lake. Just opposite the railway station, which opened in 1847, is a footpath that winds up to the top of Orrest Head (784 ft/239 m), a great viewpoint.

DANGER
BEWARE
FAST RISING TIDES
QUICKSANDS
HIDDEN CHANNELS
REN WARNS OF INCOMING TIDE
ERGENCY PHONE 999 AND ASK FOR COASTGUARD

The Southern Approaches

View from Duke's bedroom, Holker Hall

Heron Corn Mill, Beetham

Salt marsh near Flookburgh

Flat fish-shaped weathervane on Flookburgh church

Preceding page: **View across Morecambe Bay, Grange-over-Sands**

90

The Duke's bedroom, Holker Hall

Cartmel

With no lakes and much of it outside the boundary of the National Park, this area may not seem like Lakeland at all. It is very different from the other areas, with estuaries and a coastline instead of rugged landscape. But it has just as much to offer in the way of great houses, gardens and viewpoints.

The main gateway to southern Lakeland in the past was across the sands of the estuaries of the rivers Kent and Leven at low tide. The sands shift and there are large areas of quicksand, making any crossing a risky venture even when a route has been established. The routes across the sands date back to the time of the Romans and have been used regularly by locals over the centuries. The monks of Conishead Priory, near Ulverston, built an oratory halfway across the Leven estuary in the hope that prayers said for safe journeys would be answered. Earthly assistance was provided in the form of a primitive lighthouse constantly tended by a monk; the ruins of this building can be seen on the island. The monks of Cartmel Priory appointed local guides to take travellers across the Kent estuary. Since the 16th century, when the Priory was dissolved, the Duchy of Lancaster (ie, the Crown) has made the appointments. There was even a stagecoach route across the sands, with regular departures three days a week from Ulverston. Wordsworth could see this procession from his vantage point on Chapel Island, and in 1794 recorded his impressions:

'. . . . . . . .variegated crowd
Of vehicles and travellers, horse and foot,
Wading beneath the conduct of their guide. . .'

This traffic was halted by the advent of the railway in the 1850s which offered a much quicker, more convenient and less dangerous method of crossing the sands. At Grange the tidal bore comes in at 7 mph (15.6 km/h) and has claimed around 140 victims over the years. In 1821 a whole stagecoach disappeared without trace. It's said that the locals would throw dice for the belongings of any traveller who was seen setting off across the sands without a guide. One hopes this doesn't happen today, but to be sure of avoiding an outside chance of becoming an object of barter, hire a guide to take you across.

The region has a high concentration of pele towers. Those at Arnside, Hazelslack, Beetham, Dallam, Heversham, Levens and Sizergh are in very close proximity. Pele towers were built in the

View across to Arnside and its viaduct

Four views of Carnforth Steam Railway Centre

early 1300s when the English began to lose their iron grip on the Scots, who decided it was about time they got their own back. And so began a turbulent period for this prosperous area, which became a constant target of the marauding Scots. Robert the Bruce and his army paid a particularly destructive visit in 1322, rampaging down the east coast and across to Kendal before heading back northwards via Penrith.

Wilkinson monument, Lindale

The pele tower was essentially a bolt-hole that you escaped into when a raid was imminent. It was really pot-luck whether the raiders considered your tower worth the effort of a siege. Most pele towers had three storeys, no windows on the ground floor (where animals were stabled) and one low, narrow entry door reinforced with iron. The ceilings were of stone. The spiral staircase leading up to the top of the tower was narrow and easy to defend if the main door was breached. Most of the defending was done from the battlements at the top of the tower and through 'murder holes', exit points for all sorts of unspeakable missiles destined for the forces below. The pele towers were well used until the Scots were defeated in the Tudor period, finally becoming redundant in 1603 with the accession of James I to the thrones of England and Scotland.

❶ ARNSIDE

This town stands on the estuary of the River Kent. A railway line runs across the estuary, over a 50-pier viaduct, and offers a leisurely way of seeing coastal Lakeland. Just south of the town, a nature trail leads up to the viewpoint of Arnside Knott (521 ft/159 m).

❷ CARTMEL

This very attractive village is dominated by its church, the remains of a priory founded in 1188. (Open daily &) The gate-house of the priory (c 1330) was used as the local grammar school (1624–1790) and is now let by the National Trust as an art gallery and studio. (Open Apr–end Oct, Tues–Sun. Phone 05395 36602) 1½ miles north, at Broughton Lodge Farm, is Cartmel Craft Centre, which gives daily demonstrations of woodturning, calligraphy, pottery, cane furniture restoring and fabric printing. (Open Apr–end Oct, Wed–Sun &. Phone 05395 36009) Cartmel has England's smallest National Hunt race course. (Meetings held on spring and late summer Bank Hols)

❸ DOCKER PARK FARM

This working farm with horses, pigs, sheep, goats and poultry also holds exhibitions, demonstrations and has an indoor play area. (Open Easter–mid Oct daily & &. Phone 05242 21331)

❹ FLOOKBURGH

The main trade of this town is fish, especially the flat fish called fluke (hence the name Flookburgh). Even the weathervane on the local church is in the shape of a flat fish. Two popular festivals are held here: the Lakeland Rose Show in mid July and the Cumbria Steam Gathering in late July.

❺ GRANGE-OVER-SANDS

The climate here is so mild that exotic plants such as yuccas feel quite at home. Cumbria's riviera, as Grange calls itself, has a mile-long promenade and ornamental municipal gardens. The sands, after which the town gets its name, have always been treacherous and today there is still an official guide to help those people who want to cross them. Above the town, at the top of Hampsfell (727 ft/222 m), there's a small shelter for travellers. The views from here are wonderful. ⓑ 05395 34026

❻ HERON CORN MILL

Milling has gone on at Beetham since 1220. The present water-powered mill here is still in full working order. There's a picnic area here and also a museum of paper-making. (Open Easter–Sept, Tues–Sun and Bank Hols. Phone 0524 734858)

❼ HALECAT GARDEN NURSERY

This nursery near Witherslack has a small but beautiful garden created around a mid 19th-century house. It offers fine views over Morecambe Bay. (Open Mon–Fri and also Sun during summer. Phone 044852 229)

❽ HOLKER HALL

The Cavendish family (a branch of the Duke of Devonshire's line) still owns this house, which was largely rebuilt in 1874. Inside, you'll find the usual fine pictures and furniture but with the bonus of fresh flowers in every room and rope barriers in none of them. There are 25 acres of gardens, a craft and countryside exhibition, a display of Victorian, Edwardian and wartime kitchens, an adventure playground and a baby animal house. The Lakeland Motor Museum (separate admission) is within the complex of Holker Hall and has over 80 historic cars and a replica garage of the 1920s on display. (Both Hall and Motor Museum open Easter Sun–Oct, Mon–Fri and Sun & &. Phone 05395 58328)

❾ LEIGHTON HALL

The present Hall, built in the late 18th century, belongs to the Gillow family of furniture makers. The house is full of examples of their wares. Trained birds of prey, including eagles, are flown in the gardens. (Open May–Sept, Tues–Fri and Sun &. Phone 0524 734474) North-west of here, between Silverdale and Yealand Conyers, is Leighton Moss, a 300-acre RSPB reserve set among meres, reeds and willows. The visitors' centre has a shop, video, tea room and display area. (Open daily; facilities closed Tues. Phone 0524 701601) The Morecambe Bay Bird Sanctuary nearby (just off the Warton to Silverdale road) is an excellent spot for flocks of waders. (No facilities)

❿ LEVENS HALL

This great Elizabethan house was built round a 13th-century pele tower. It's most noted for its gardens (laid out in 1692), especially the topiary, but there's plenty else besides, including an adventure playground and a collection of working steam engines (also steam traction engines on Sundays). The house contains some fine pieces of furniture, paintings and, if you're very sharp-eyed, ghosts. (Open Easter Sun–end Sept, Sun–Thurs. & Phone 05395 60321)

⓫ LINDALE

The most important feature in this village is a 40-foot (12 m) cast-iron obelisk standing on the B road to Grange. It was ordered by John Wilkinson (1728–1808) as part of his funeral arrangements, which also included a cast-iron coffin. Wilkinson had helped cast the first iron bridge and had launched the first iron ship. 'Iron Mad' John, as he was called, was originally buried in his garden at Castle Head, just outside the village, with the obelisk erected over his grave. Later his coffin was removed to the local churchyard and the obelisk re-erected at its present site.

⓬ STEAMTOWN RAILWAY CENTRE

Situated at Carnforth, Steamtown has around 30 diesel and steam engines ranging in size from a giant express to a tiny tank engine. You can also see coaches, a signal box, a coaling plant and miniature and model railways. (Open Easter–Oct daily. Minimal facilities in winter. Phone 0524 732100 for details of when the engines or the miniature railway are working) Next door is Carnforth railway station where David Lean's classic 'weepie' *Brief Encounter*, with Trevor Howard and Celia Johnson was filmed.